Celebrations
with
Carmela's Cucina

Celebrations
with
Carmela's Cucina

ൠ

Carmela Hobbins

Photography by Erica Loeks

Wine pairings by Robert Hobbins

NODIN PRESS

Design: John Toren
Food Photography: Erica Loeks
Cover photos: Erica Loeks

additional photo credits:
Carmela Hobbins – 18,43, 45, 84, 98, 102, 113, 114, 119,120, 132, 133, 134, 135, 137, 146, 152;
Katrin Egger, 70; Doris Fortino, 85; Tish Osborn, 94; Bob Hobbins, 99; Gerry Stebbins, 106; Jessica Akin Hobbins, 108.
Grapevine border © mist / fotolia.com. Page 27 photo © Svetlana Kolpakoval / dreamstime.com.
Page 29 photo © Michel Mota Da Cruz / dreamstime.com. Page 33 photo © Avevstaf / dreamstime.com.
Page 43 photo © Dwight Smith / dreamstime.com. Page 89 photo © Jinlide / dreamstime.com.

ISBN 978-1-935666-26-4
Library of Congress Control Number: 2011937558

Nodin Press
530 North Third Street
Suite 120
Minneapolis, MN
55401

For all of the men in my life—my sons Brian, Patrick and Teddy, and my wonderful husband Bob. You have loved and encouraged me every day and have happily eaten all of the many recipes that have been tested on you for years.

You each make every day a celebration. Thank you!

Acknowledgements

With gratitude and appreciation, I wish to thank the many friends, acquaintances, and family members who have tirelessly assisted me with *Celebrations with Carmela's Cucina*.

Recipe testing can be hard work, but the reward comes in sharing a delicious meal with family and friends when you're done. Many thanks to Annie Dingerson, Connie Mertz, Peggy McGillan, Lorraine Orbon, Peggy Tolbert, Marla Borer, Mary Ann Fenlon, Terry Sweatman, Jenny Johnson, Sandy Nelson, Kathy Foggia, Tish Osborn, Christina Sheran, Jane Hulbert, Joan Holthaus, Betty Olson, Cathy Schneeman, Diane Angelo, Patty Tucker and Phyllis Kohler. Because of their suggestions, proof-reading and improvements to the recipes, *Celebrations with Carmela's Cucina* is a better cookbook.

Close friends and dear family members from as near as across the street and as far away as Italy shared some of their favorite recipes for parts of this book, and these recipes are now among my favorites, too. My appreciation goes to Suzie Swenson, Michele Manatt, Susan Tewksbury, Vincenza Alessio, Bob Wehage, Susan Lukens, Jackie Lokkesmoe, Frances Grazianao, Julie McHugh, Sarah Tursi, Doris Fortino, and Daniela Grossi. Thanks also to Ed Noonan for allowing us to take photos on the grounds of the beautiful Brownstones on France.

Many thanks to my brother Bob Tursi, his wife, Amy, and my nephew, R.J., for sharing with all of us the most popular recipes from the Latin King restaurant in Des Moines, Iowa.

Thank you to my daughter-in-law, Jessica, who introduced me to Erica Loeks. Erica worked patiently for hours, week after week, styling and photographing the food I prepared. Not only is Erica an outstanding photographer, she is a relentless perfectionist who made my food *look* as good as it tastes. Her creative ideas for food art appear throughout the pages of this book.

I thank you, John Toren, for your creative ideas and suggestions as editor of this book. Thank you Norton Stillman for agreeing to publish *Celebrations with Carmela's Cucina* and for your genuine friendship over many years.

Finally, to Bob Hobbins, my wonderful husband of 38 years, I want to express my love and gratitude, which you so richly deserve. Thank you for continually encouraging me throughout this project. When I was down, you lifted me up. When I couldn't make it to the market, you brought home what I needed. You washed the dishes and moved the furniture during photo shoots—and then put it all back in place. You have been with me every step of the way, editing, critiquing and praising my work. The creative wine and beer pairings you compiled make each section a more complete celebration. It was great fun sampling the wine and beers with you while trying out old and new recipes until we felt that we got things just right. It has been a wonderful journey!

Contents

Introduction   *ix*

New Year's Day Buffet   14

Romantic Valentine's Day Dinner   24

Carnivale   32

Easter Lunch   40

Mother's Day Brunch   50

Father's Day   60

Dinner *al Fresco*   70

Fourth of July   78

Lunch in the Garden   86

Dinner at Tursi's Latin King   96

Thanksgiving   102

Christmas Eve   116

Christmas Day   128

New Year's Eve   138

recipe index   147

In Memory of My Father
Joseph S. Tursi

No one loved a party or celebration more than my father, Joe Tursi. Born in Terravecchia, Italy in 1921, he immigrated to the United States when he was eight years old, following his parents, Carmela Pigneri Tursi and Francesco Tursi. His first job was as a shoeshine boy, and he built a clothing business with his brother Paul that became one of the largest independent clothing stores in the Midwest. He and my mother, Sarah Fazio Tursi, were married for over 60 years. He proposed on the 4th of July, with patriotic music and fireworks as the back drop for his "big question." Mom said, "Yes," leading to a lifetime of celebrations.

In his retirement, he continued to work as a volunteer and was the lunchtime host at the Latin King Restaurant, where he greeted each customer with a smile, handshake or a great big hug and kiss. Every baby was the most beautiful for him; each young lady, his best girl; and every man, woman or child who passed his way was his best friend. Dad loved them all, and was beloved by all in return.

His life was guided by a few simple philosophies: Always be a gentleman, never go to sleep angry at the ones you love, family first, and work harder than everyone else around you. These simple rules led him to accomplish many great things, and his legacy lives on in the organizations he founded, the many friends he made, and in his greatest pleasure—his family. He lived out those basic rules in all of his relationships, providing a lesson to us all.

Dad's beginnings were very humble, and that is the way he lived his life. But Dad did love a party or a celebration and was always dreaming up a way to bring people together to enjoy each other's company. He began his day by turning on the radio and singing in the morning, and he continued to sing all day. Each family dinner began with a prayer and a request that we would always be around for each of the parties that my mother and he continued to host until the year that he passed away. Then he would pick up his wine glass and toast us all.

Thanks, Dad, for all you taught me, for being the best father, counselor and friend any child could ask for, and for continuing the celebration in heaven. SALUTE!

introduction

I grew up in a big Italian family where it seemed there was always a reason to celebrate something special. It began with a baby's baptism and the celebration that followed to welcome that new little person into the fold. Then there were the parties that followed the administration of all of the sacraments. There were also holidays, birthdays, anniversaries, and many other special events to be commemorated by celebration with family, friends and, of course, special food and wine.

My role as hostess began when I was just sixteen years old. I invited about twenty-five of my closest friends and their dates to a "coketail party" before a high school dance. Actually I hosted many of those parties during my high school years. As I recall, red punch and small sandwiches were always served. We held these parties in my parents' rec room, where they chaperoned us vigilantly as we shyly made small talk with our dates before leaving for the dance. At one such party I was terribly sick with laryngitis. I could barely whisper, but the party went on, and everyone had a great time.

Soon we were seniors in high school and, of course, I served on the social committee for every dance held at our all-girls' school, St. Joseph Academy in Des Moines, Iowa. Decorating the cavernous Val-Air Ballroom or the Hotel Fort Des Moines was a challenge I loved. Today, parents spend months organizing an extravagant party for their teens after graduation or senior prom. I organized a bowling party for all of my friends after our prom and a picnic the following day.

After graduating from college I lived with two roommates, Martha and Lynn, in an apartment in Omaha, Nebraska, where the pattern continued. We would frequently prepare lavish meals, crafted from recipes in gourmet magazines, and invite our friends over for a party or a bridal shower. We decorated our cozy apartment, tried out new recipes, served "Cold Duck" wine, and saw ourselves as very sophisticated hostesses.

As a young bride, I registered for silver, china, crystal and fancy table linens. I was sure that I would be hosting many elegant dinner parties for our friends, family, clients and colleagues. And I was absolutely correct. I used to spend weeks preparing for these events, consulting books written by Julia Child and entertainment guides by Martha Stewart. I always followed the recipes and suggestions to the letter!

I liked entertaining and gourmet cooking so much that, with my friend Marla Borer, I created Occasions Catering. I was quite happy catering other peoples' events and celebrations, while hosting my own as well. Marla and I especially loved doing cocktail parties and small weddings. But as our families grew, so did our own personal entertaining commitments. After four years, we dissolved our company so we could concentrate on our own celebrations.

For years, my husband Bob and I hosted an annual holiday open house for friends and neighbors to benefit one of our local charities. I would bake desserts and cookies, make candy, and prepare our home to accommodate 200 plus people on the second Sunday in December. Then, a few weeks later, we would invite our close friends for a New Year's Eve celebration that included a multi-course dinner with wine pairings. During the remainder of the year, we would celebrate the holidays, mark special occasions, and periodically get together with friends for a big bash.

In the past I would do all of the cooking, cleaning and serving myself. I learned to prepare menus that could be made ahead, so I could enjoy my own parties. After all, the reason you invite people to join you for a celebration is so you can spend time with them, rather than being stuck in the kitchen.

More recently, I have been teaching cooking classes professionally and leading culinary tours to Italy and Savannah, Georgia. My entertaining has become more relaxed as a result. We still enjoy having friends over, but now instead of spending weeks in preparation for an event, I give our guests a drink and a little antipasti when they arrive and invite everyone into the kitchen to help me cook or at least keep me company while I finish dinner. My guests enjoy being part of the preparations, and I enjoy the company. Then we can all sit down together and enjoy a long, leisurely meal.

The menus, recipes and wine pairings in this book follow the calendar year and are intended to make entertaining fun and easy for you and special for your guests. Bob has worked diligently (and sipped more than a few glasses of wine) to bring you a wide selection of pairings that work beautifully with the food. Many of the recipes are taken from my culinary classes and tours and, according to my clients and guests, are proven winners.

From the easy New Year's Day Buffet to the elegant New Year's Eve Dinner, there is something here for everyone. Invite your special "Valentine" for dinner and treat him/her to an elegant evening, which you can prepare well in advance. Get the kids to help you prepare the Mother's Day Brunch, and make Mom feel like queen for the day.

Dine "al fresco," as we do in Italy, and serve wine from Bob's suggestions. You will feel like you are in a Chianti vineyard without the expensive airfare. And Dad will feel extra special while enjoying a dinner that includes recipes from my favorite Italian trattoria, La Sostanza. Entertain your guests casually as we do on the 4th of July at Big Sand Lake with a Shrimp Boil and a Red, White and Blue Lemon Curd Tart. This menu is easy and fun, leaving plenty of time to enjoy a parade, boat ride, or a dip in the lake.

Carmela and Bob with friends at the Brownstones of France in Edina, Minnesota.

In the fall, give thanks with our extra-special Thanksgiving menu, including the best smoked turkey I have ever eaten. Just be ready to receive the multitude of compliments that will come your way. Remember to invite someone who may otherwise be alone to share this special day with you.

For me the Christmas holidays will always be particularly significant. The Feast of the Seven Fish, which Italians annually observe, reminds me of my roots and of my own grandmothers and mother who introduced me to this tradition. Even those who normally shy away from fish will find something to like in this unique meal.

Much of the entertaining that Bob and I do now involves celebrations centered upon the marriages of our sons, Brian, Patrick and Teddy, their brides, friends and extended family. We find ourselves hosting many engagement parties, bridal showers and groom's dinners. Many of the menus in this book are appropriate for these events.

I love a party, and I have so many wonderful reasons to celebrate. As you can see, I have been doing it all of my life. With the birth of our granddaughter, Lillian Sarah, I can be assured that these celebrations of life will continue into the next generation of our family.

a word about wine pairings / robert hobbins

At the outset, there are two important things to understand about pairing food and drink: First, the process of pairing presents questions to which there are no "right" answers; some are merely better than others. It is ultimately a matter of individual taste and personal enjoyment. Second, this process should never cease to be fun. There will necessarily be some trial and error involved, and what could be more enjoyable than the "practice" sessions?

It seems that we are born with some basic sense for pairings. How old were you when it dawned on you that nothing went better with a still-warm chocolate chip cookie than a glass of fresh milk? First we realize that these two things taste great together. A bit later we come to recognize that each tastes better in combination with the other than it does by itself. Our list of favorite pairings has begun! This list expands as our diet becomes more diverse. A cup of fresh-brewed tea is the perfect companion to a raisin scone; there is nothing like a cold beer with a grilled bratwurst—and so it goes.

We believe that it is helpful to think of the drink you select for a meal as a sauce or a seasoning for the food involved. It should complement the

food rather than compete with it for center stage. We have learned this approach from the wonderful people of Italy (and who has given more careful thought to food and drink over the centuries than the Italians?). Italians rarely drink wine without a bit of food, and seldom have a meal without a glass of wine. For them, food and wine are like an old married couple—always together and always playing to one another's strengths. When wine and food work that way together, the enjoyment of the two merge into a larger sensation we call "a wonderful meal."

When planning a meal, it is certainly possible to begin with the drink, especially if you have a cherished bottle of wine in the cellar or a new favorite beer you want to showcase. However, in most cases it works better to begin by selecting the foods to be offered. Then, with menu in hand, you can consider the courses to be included, the key ingredients, the seasonings and condiments to be used, and even the time of year in selecting the drink that will "fit."

We are blessed to live in a time and place where the variety of wonderful foods and beverages available for us to enjoy year around is truly incredible. American consumers have access to wines from all over the world, to an ever-expanding collection of craft beers, and to a large array of exotic coffees and teas. At times the sheer number of choices can seem almost overwhelming.

At that point we need to remind ourselves that this business of pairing need not be overly complicated. A few basic principles can help narrow the range of options considerably. First, there is the tried and true adage, "If it grows together, it goes together." Think about where the dishes featured in the meal come from, then consider the wines, beers or other beverages that are native to that same area. The Sangiovese di Romagna of Bologna seems to have been predestined to accompany pasta in a Bolognese ragu; a Rosé de Provence partners beautifully with salad niçoise or a spicy bouillabaisse. I am not sure precisely why this is so, but the adage is very reliable.

Another useful approach involves testing the aroma and taste of the drink you have in mind in advance to see if you detect any of the aromas or flavors that will appear in the food you are preparing. If you do, your proposed pairing will probably work well. Try consulting with nearby wine bar or wine shop staff, who usually have valuable insights to share. Carmela and I often take a recipe along to our favorite shops to consult in detail. Over time, this can dramatically expand your knowledge and your pairings horizons.

Finally, there are reference books available for those who wish to pursue the subject of pairings more avidly, or who are faced with the challenge of finding a drink pairing for a dish that is unique and unfamiliar. Our favorite is *What to Drink with What You Eat*, by Andrew Dornenburg and Karen Page. The range of foods and beverages covered in this work is remarkable, and it has an outstanding index that allows you find pairings, whether you start with the food you have in mind or the drink you would like to consider. This handy volume is even available as an app.

We also make frequent use of *Vino Italiano: The Regional Wines of Italy*, written by Joseph Bastianich and David Lynch. Not only does this represent the definitive collection on Italian wines, conveniently arranged by region and filled with pairings suggestions, but it also includes a wealth of excellent recipes provided by the iconic Italian chefs Lydia Bastianich and Mario Batali.

Our closing observation on pairings is simply that a good pairing of food and drink is not dependent upon the cost of either. Drinking a fine French Bordeaux with a pizza will not enhance the enjoyment of either. A spicy California Zinfandel at a fraction of the price of the Bordeaux would be a much better choice. The great majority of the wines we recommend here may be purchased for $20 per bottle or less. None of the craft beers we suggest are unduly expensive. A great pairing is not a function of what you spend, but the thought you give to your selection.

OLIVE BAR

BAGNA CAUDA WITH FRESH VEGETABLES

MARINATED SHRIMP ON SKEWERS

STROMBOLI OF ITALIAN MEATS AND CHEESES

TURKEY SOUP IN BREAD BOWLS

TOMATO VEGETABLE SOUP

LENTIL SOUP WITH SWEET ITALIAN SAUSAGE

COCONUT JOYS

CASHEW CLUSTERS

New Year's Day sets the tone for the whole year, so keep it simple, relaxed and—most of all—fun. Many of us have been feasting since Thanksgiving, and we're looking for something a bit lighter for this first day of the year. Last night you entertained your friends (or were entertained yourself) in grand style. Now it's time for something less elegant, but still delicious. If you have holiday guests, give everyone a recipe to work on, and this buffet will come together easily. Then enjoy the fruits of your collective labor while watching a bowl game or a movie, playing cards, or just relaxing together.

Have plenty of wine, beer, soft drinks, bottled water, juices, and coffee on hand. And for those who may have had just a little too much celebrating the night before, keep a bottle of aspirin handy.

A relaxed party like this will serve about 20 and is done "open house" style, with your guests eating when they want. I have the soups going in a crockpot or on the stove; everything else is served at room-temperature in the kitchen so that guests can help themselves. Several televisions are set up around the house so friends and family can choose where they want to eat and what movie or bowl game they want to watch. (This menu would be great for Super Bowl Sunday or another winter occasion!)

bagna cauda

Bagna Cauda comes from the Piedmont area of northern Italy. In that mountainous region a simple warm fondue of extra virgin olive oil and anchovies coats raw vegetables and bread sticks, transforming them into tasty morsels for all to enjoy.

½ cup extra virgin olive oil
2 sticks (½ pound) butter
4 cloves of garlic, crushed
1 small can of anchovies, well drained
½ to 1 teaspoon freshly ground black pepper
Crushed red pepper to taste
Grissini (Italian bread sticks) or loaf of
    crusty Italian bread, cubed
An assortment of fresh raw vegetables cut into
    bite-sized pieces, for example:
1 pound bag small carrots
1 pound whole mushrooms, cleaned
1 head broccoli
1 head cauliflower
2 fennel bulbs
1 bag celery
2 red peppers, cut into strips
2 yellow peppers, cut into strips
2 bundles scallions

In a heavy pot or over a double boiler, add the olive oil and butter, stirring until the butter is melted.

olive bar

Most grocery stores these days offer a terrific assortment of olives. I suggest that you choose three to five different kinds of olives for your own olive bar. Purchase about a half-pound of each selection, then pile them into a divided bowl or serving tray. Some olive bars also include roasted peppers and marinated artichoke hearts; those items would also make a wonderful addition to your olive bar.

Once the butter is melted, add the crushed garlic, the drained anchovies, and both black and red pepper. Stir all together and simmer until the anchovies melt into the butter/olive oil mixture. Transfer the dip to a fondue pot with a candle to keep the mixture warm. Meanwhile, cube bread, wash and cut vegetables into serving pieces, and arrange them around the fondue pot.

– serves 8-12

marinated shrimp skewers

Purchase the freshest and largest shrimp your budget will permit for these easy, tasty skewers. Your guests are going to love them, and they will never guess that it took you just minutes to prepare them.

60 medium-sized raw shrimp, cleaned and
　　deveined
1 cup minced onion
1 teaspoon Kosher salt
2 teaspoons finely minced garlic
2 teaspoons dried oregano
1 teaspoon dried basil
1 teaspoon dried thyme
6 tablespoons freshly squeezed lemon juice

1 cup canola oil
20 bamboo skewers

Clean and rinse shrimp and pat dry. In a bowl mix together the onion, garlic, salt, herbs, lemon juice and oil. Add shrimp to the bowl and marinate for 20-30 minutes.

While the shrimp are marinating, soak the bamboo skewers in water for 10 minutes. Drain the skewers and shrimp, then thread 3 shrimp on the end of each skewer. Pre-heat the oven to 400 degrees. Place the skewers in a single layer on a baking sheet lined with foil or parchment paper. Roast shrimp until just opaque—about 8-10 minutes. Line a round platter with salad greens or kale and arrange warm skewers in spoke fashion.

– makes 20 skewers

stromboli of meat, cheese, and pesto dipping sauce

To *feed 20 people you may want to make 3 of these stromboli. Select a number of different cooked or cured Italian meats and cheeses to provide a variety of flavors. Purchase a good quality pesto sauce from the dairy case, or make your own during the summer, when herbs are plentiful. Freeze your home-made pesto in one-half pint containers and bring it to room temperature when ready to serve. If you want something warm to dip your stromboli, heat up some of your favorite marinara sauce.*

    1 carton of refrigerated pizza dough
        (traditional style works best)
    ¼ pound of your choice of cooked or cured
        Italian meats, thinly sliced
    ¼ pound of your choice of Italian cheese,
        thinly sliced
    ½ cup prepared pesto sauce
    2 tablespoons melted butter
    Pesto or marinara sauce for dipping

Unroll pizza dough onto a jelly roll pan lined with parchment paper. Spread ½ cup of prepared pesto onto dough. Layer meats and cheese on top of the pesto. Carefully roll the pizza dough from the long end jelly-roll style, making sure the seam is on the bottom and the ends are tucked under and sealed well. Brush the top with the melted butter and bake at 400 degrees for 10 minutes or until the top is golden brown and pizza crust is well baked. Let cool for about five minutes and cut into slices. Arrange on a platter and serve with the dipping sauces.

– serves 8

turkey vegetable soup in mini-bread bowls

*T*his soup has always been a family favorite, but using a new twist—ground turkey—makes it a much healthier version than my original recipe, which called for ground beef. The best part is that you get to eat the bowl that holds the soup. Double this recipe to feed your gang of guests, making at least one soup bowl per person. If, by chance, there is any soup left over, divide it into lunch- or dinner-sized portions and freeze it. Make the bread bowls a day ahead and store them in an airtight container until needed.

1 pound ground turkey
¼ teaspoon Lawry's Seasoning Salt
¼ teaspoon freshly ground pepper
1 cup chopped onion
1½ cups chopped celery
1 cup thinly sliced carrots
2 cups of diced potatoes
4 cups best quality chicken stock
3 tablespoons of tomato paste with
    Italian herbs
1 (14 ounce) can of diced tomatoes with
    Italian herbs
1 (10 ounce) package of frozen corn kernels
1 bay leaf
Parmesan cheese, grated

In a large soup pot, brown the ground turkey, season with salt and pepper, add onions, celery and carrots and continue to brown with the turkey. Drain well. Return meat and vegetables to the pot and stir in all remaining ingredients. Bring to a simmer. Cover pot and cook soup until the vegetables are tender crisp—about 30 minutes.

soup bowls

2 packages Pillsbury Grand Home
    Style Biscuits
Pam cooking spray

While the soup is simmering, prepare the bread bowls. Turn cupcake pans upside down and spray well with Pam cooking spray. Remove biscuits from their package and carefully stretch over the upturned cupcake pans, using every other pan. Bake according to package directions. When nicely browned, remove the pans from the oven. When the bowls are cool enough to handle, trim off the bottom of the bowl if necessary so that it will sit level on the plate. Ladle soup into the mini-bread bowl and top with Parmesan cheese.

– serves 10-12

tomato vegetable soup

This is a very hearty and delicious soup, which is easy to prepare and freezes well. Do not let the long list of ingredients keep you from making this soup. You will find most of what you need already on hand in a well-stocked refrigerator and pantry. The recipe was given to me by one of my college friends, Michelle Manatt, and I have been using it in a popular Soups class that I teach every January. Make sure to offer freshly grated Parmesan cheese to garnish a piping hot bowl of this tasty soup.

¼ cup butter
1 small garlic clove, minced
1 small onion, chopped
1 large potato, shredded
1 small carrot, shredded
1 small zucchini, shredded
1 stalk celery, chopped
1 (28 ounce) can Italian tomatoes
2 tablespoons flour
1 tablespoon brown sugar
2 cups of chicken broth
½ teaspoon basil
½ teaspoon marjoram
1 bay leaf
1 cup 2% milk
¼ teaspoon curry powder
¼ teaspoon paprika
Salt and pepper to taste
Parmesan cheese, grated

In a large soup pot, melt the butter. Then add the garlic, onion, potato, carrot, zucchini and celery. Sauté until the vegetables are slightly wilted. Meanwhile, in a food processor, chop the tomatoes with their juice. Sprinkle 2 tablespoons of flour over the vegetable mixture and stir until the flour is blended into the vegetables --about 2 minutes. Add the chopped tomatoes, brown sugar, chicken broth, basil, marjoram and bay leaf. Cover and simmer the soup for 20 minutes. At that point, remove the bay leaf and add the milk, curry powder, paprika and salt and pepper. Stir well, then simmer for an additional 5 minutes to let the soup warm and thicken. Add Parmesan cheese to each bowl of soup at serving time.

– serves 10-12

✦

CARMELA COMMENTS | This soup is even better the next day, after the flavors have had a chance to blend. It doubles easily and freezes well.

lentil soup with spicy italian sausage

Italian culture is filled with curious food traditions. Certain foods must be eaten only on a single holiday; others are believed to provide some unique health benefit or to bring you good luck. And so it is with lentils. Although beans and lentils are actually considered "poor man's food," the shape of the round lentil loosely resembles a coin. Tradition holds that eating lentils on New Year's Day will ensure that you have a prosperous year. And the more lentils you eat, the more prosperous you will be. This colorful recipe is full of fiber, low in calories, and delicious. So dish up a big bowl of this thick soup and eat your way to health and wealth!

2 tablespoons olive oil
1 pound fully cooked sweet Italian sausage, crumbled
¼ pound of pancetta, cubed
1 large onion, chopped
2 large carrots, peeled and chopped
2 large stalks of celery, chopped
2½ teaspoons dried Italian seasoning blend
1 pound of brown lentils
1 (6 ounce) can of tomato paste with Italian herbs
6 cups of low salt chicken broth
1 (5 ounce) package of baby spinach leaves

In a large heavy soup pot, warm the olive oil over medium heat, add the sausage and pancetta, and cook until well browned while stirring occasionally—about 7-10 minutes. Using a slotted spoon, transfer the sausage and pancetta to a clean bowl. Add onion, carrots, celery and Italian seasonings to the drippings in the pot. Cook until the onion is translucent and vegetables begin to soften—about 7-8 minutes—stirring often. Add the lentils and stir to coat. Add the tomato paste and stir into the vegetables and lentils. Add 4 cups of the broth and bring the soup to a boil. Then reduce the heat to a simmer until the lentils are tender—about 30-40 minutes. Stir the soup occasionally, adding more broth by ¼ cupful as needed if the soup is getting too thick. When the lentils are tender, add the sausage and pancetta and simmer for an additional 10 to 20 minutes. Season the soup with salt and pepper. Just before serving, stir in the spinach. Cook until the spinach is wilted—about 3 minutes.

– serves 8

✦

CARMELA COMMENTS | Hot Italian sausage can be used instead of the sweet Italian sausage, and smoked bacon could be substituted for the pancetta. I like the spinach in this soup, but other greens such as kale or escarole could also be used.

coconut joys

I first came across this recipe when our neighborhood book club had a Christmas cookie exchange. My neighbor, Jackie Lokesmo, brought Coconut Joys to share, and we all loved them. I asked Jackie for the recipe, and she was happy to oblige. At Christmas time I decorate the top of this candy-like cookie with "Red Hot" candies. Everyone is going to love these cookies, so make plenty in advance and freeze them, leaving one less thing to prepare the day of your party.

½ cup (1 stick) butter
2 cups confectioners' sugar
3 cups shredded coconut
12-16 ounces melted semi-sweet
    chocolate chips
Red Hot candies (optional)

Melt butter in a saucepan. Remove the pan from heat and add the confectioners' sugar and coconut. Mix everything together very well. Shape rounded teaspoons of the coconut mixture into balls. Using the end of a wooden spoon, make a dent in the top of each ball. Put chocolate chips in a glass bowl and heat in a microwave at medium power. Every 30 seconds stop the microwave and stir the chocolate until it is melted, smooth and shiny. With a very small spoon, fill the indentation in the cookie with the melted chocolate and top with the Red Hots.

– makes 3 dozen

✦

CARMELA COMMENTS | You can also transfer the chocolate to a small zip lock bag. Seal the bag and cut a very small hole in one tip in order to pipe the chocolate into the center of the cookie.

cashew clusters

For years I made these easy clusters using peanuts. Then I switched over to cashews and love them, but you could use just about any nut you like. These candies make a great hostess gift too; just put a dozen in a cellophane holiday bag and tie the bag with a pretty ribbon. Anyone would be thrilled to get such a delicious gift. This recipe can easily be doubled.

    12 ounces chocolate chips
    12 ounces butterscotch chips
    2 cups cashews

Melt the chips in a double boiler, making sure no water gets into the upper pan. When the chips are completely melted add the cashews and stir well.

Line a jellyroll pan with waxed or parchment paper and drop the mixture by the teaspoonful onto the pan. Put the pan in the refrigerator to set up the clusters. These freeze well.

– makes 3 dozen

Wine Pairings

This is a great menu to savor with a nice Chianti wine from Tuscany. This time-honored blend based on the Sangiovese grape will enhance the seasoned meats and cheese in the stromboli, while complementing the soups as well. It is not necessary to pay for a premium Chianti Riserva to enjoy this meal; rather, a more approachable Chianti will do nicely. Labels that we enjoy include the Ruffino Chiantis, those from Verrazano, and the reliable Badia a Coltibuono "RS" Chianti.

Another nice offering for your guests at this buffet would be an India Pale Ale, which certainly has the body to match well with these foods. Summit Brewing makes a nice IPA or, with the right group, you might try Flying Dog Brewery's Belgian-style IPA called "Raging Bitch" (their name, not mine!). Finally, as a special treat for your beer-drinking friends, consider the "Two-Hearted Ale" from Bell's.

Romantic Valentine's Day Dinner

BAKED STUFFED BRIE

GREEN SALAD WITH PEAR, WALNUTS

AND GORGONZOLA CHEESE

BEEFSTEAK WELLINGTON WITH WINE

AND MUSHROOM SAUCE

DUCHESS POTATOES

BEAUTIFUL VEGETABLE PLATTER

RED VELVET VALENTINE'S DAY CUPCAKES

Valentine's Day is one of the most romantic days of the year, and many couples enjoy dining at a special restaurant on that day. I prefer to dine at home, where I can share a loving evening with the special person in my life, my husband Bob, and just a few very close friends. We find it much more enjoyable eating in the peace and quiet of our own dining room on this special day, rather than taking on the long lines, big crowds, and often-harried wait staff of a restaurant.

I do go all out on Valentine's Day, however, using my best silver, china, crystal, and linens. I like to have several fresh floral arrangement positioned here and there around the house, saving beautiful red roses for the dining table.

Since much of this meal can be made ahead of time, it's also largely stress free, so you have plenty of time to share with your Valentine and guests. Ask everyone to dress up, open some wonderful wine, light the candles and build a cozy fire. Have your favorite love songs playing in the background and make sure that the babysitter keeps the children well entertained and gets them to bed early.

baked stuffed brie

My friend Suzie Swenson gave me this recipe years ago after serving it one evening at our Wood Hill Book Club. I've made it many times since to great acclaim. Pears could be substituted for the apples and walnuts for the almonds.

I arrange the cheese on a lovely platter. The apple, almonds, and Craisins overflow from the cheese, making a very pretty presentation. Arrange crackers or baguette slices around the cheese and fresh fruit around the platter for an added festive touch.

1 large round of Brie cheese
½ cup of chopped and peeled green apple
¼ cup sliced almonds
¼ cup dried Craisins
1 tablespoon packed brown sugar
¼ teaspoon cinnamon
1 tablespoon melted butter
French baguette or crackers

Mix together chopped green apple, sliced almonds, Craisins, brown sugar and cinnamon. Melt the butter and gently fold it with the other ingredients. Cut cheese horizontally in half and place bottom round of cheese on a pie plate or other oven-safe

◆

CARMELA COMMENTS | When slicing the cheese make sure that it's very cold. The fruit and nut mixture for this recipe can be doubled; it will spill out from between the pieces of cheese and add to the beauty of the presentation.

dish. Place half of the mixture on the cut side of the cheese. Replace the top of cheese and cover with the remaining mixture. Bake at 350 degrees for 15 to 20 minutes. Serve with a thinly sliced baguette or crackers. Garnish with more fruit.

green salad with pears, walnuts and gorgonzola cheese

This is a very versatile salad. Change the greens around as you like. Apple or strawberries could be used instead of the pear, and pecans or almonds could be substituted for the walnuts. Goat cheese would be very good if you'd like to use something other than Gorgonzola.

8 cups of assorted field greens
2 unpeeled pears, sliced
½ cup toasted walnuts
½ cup crumbled Gorgonzola Cheese

dressing

¾ cup extra virgin olive oil
¼ cup balsamic vinegar
¼ teaspoon salt
1 garlic clove, crushed

Whisk all of the dressing ingredients until well emulsified. Toast the walnuts on a jellyroll pan at 350 degrees for about 6-7 minutes. Set aside and cool.

At serving time, in a large bowl combine lettuce, pears and walnuts. Toss well, coating all of the leaves of the lettuce. Serve on individual chilled plates and top each serving with Gorgonzola cheese.

– serves 8

beefsteak wellington

I love these bundles of elegance, and one of the best things is that you can make them ahead of time and freeze them. On the day of your party just remove them from the freezer about 30 minutes before baking time. You can welcome your guests feeling relaxed and stress free, knowing that they are going to be wowed with this special entrée.

1 17¼-ounce package frozen puff pasty
   (2 sheets)
8 (5 ounce) beef tenderloin steaks, cut
   1-inch thick
1 tablespoon cooking oil
5 ounces of liver pate (from the deli or make
   your own)
¼ cup breadcrumbs
1 tablespoon chopped flat leaf parsley
½ teaspoon dried basil
¼ teaspoon garlic salt
Dash of pepper

Thaw pastry according to package directions. In a large skillet brown the steaks in hot oil over medium-high heat for 1 minute on each side. Drain steaks on paper towels. Cool. Stir together remaining ingredients and spread a rounded tablespoon of pate mixture on top of each steak. Roll each sheet of puff pastry into an 11-inch square; cut each sheet into four equal pieces. Place pastry squares on top of steaks and fold under the steaks, trimming pastry so only ½-inch remains folded under the meat. Reserve any pastry trimmings, and using a heart shaped cookie cutter, cut out shapes and place on top of tenderloin bundles using a bit of water to moisten hearts so that they will stick. Place bundles on a cookie sheet, cover and freeze for an hour or more. When bundles are frozen they may be placed in plastic freezer bags until ready to use.

To serve, place frozen bundles pastry-side up on a rack in a shallow baking pan. Bake uncovered in a 450-degree oven for about 25 minutes or until pastry is nicely browned. You may need to loosely cover the bundles the last few minutes of baking.

– serves 8

✦

CARMELA COMMENTS | If you would like, double the sauce for this recipe so you have more to pass around the table.

wine and mushroom sauce

1 cup sliced fresh mushrooms
¼ cup sliced green onions
4 tablespoons butter
½ cup beef stock, separated
½ cup dry red wine
4 teaspoons cornstarch
Salt and pepper to taste

In a medium sauté pan cook mushrooms and onions in butter until tender. Add the beef stock, reserving ¼ cup. Stir cornstarch into ¼ cup of the reserved stock until dissolved, and add it to the sauté pan. Cook the mixture 1 to 2 minutes, making sure the cornstarch is cooked into the mixture. Add wine, stir, and cook until thick and bubbly. Add salt and pepper, then cook and stir a few minutes more. Serve with the steak bundles.

– serves 8

duchess potatoes

Duchess Potatoes are easy to make and very pretty on a dinner plate. Freshly grated nutmeg is worth the extra effort, as it adds a bit of color and great taste. I sometimes double or triple the recipe and freeze the mounds so I have Duchess Potatoes whenever I want a fast side-dish.

2 cups hot mashed potatoes
¼ cup butter, divided
2 - 2½ tablespoons light cream
1 egg
Several dashes of freshly ground nutmeg
¼ teaspoon salt

Beat together the hot potatoes, 2 tablespoons butter, cream, egg, nutmeg and ¼ teaspoon salt together. Line a baking sheet with parchment paper. Using a pastry bag with a large star tip, pipe mixture into 8 mounds. Freeze until firm and put potato mounds into a freezer bag.

To serve, place frozen mounds on a greased cookie sheet. Melt remaining butter and brush onto the mounds. Grate more nutmeg over the top. Bake uncovered in a 375 degree oven for 20 to 25 minutes or until heated through

– serves 8

beautiful vegetable platter

This recipe can be modified to serve any number of people. Vary the vegetables depending on the season and what you most enjoy eating.

½ head cauliflower cut into flowerets
2 stalks broccoli cut into flowerets
2 carrots sliced into ¼ inch slices
1 yellow pepper cut into ½ inch squares
1 red pepper cut into ½ inch squares
½ pint cherry tomatoes

1 medium summer squash cut into
    ¾-inch slices
⅓ cup extra virgin olive oil
1 teaspoon garlic salt
Freshly ground black pepper to taste
¼ cup freshly grated Parmesan cheese

Heat oven to 450 degrees. Prepare the vegetables and in a bowl toss them with the olive oil, garlic salt and pepper. Transfer to a baking sheet and roast for 20 minutes. Stir once during roasting. Place cooked vegetables on a platter and sprinkle with the cheese.

– serves 8

red velvet valentine's cupcakes

Red cake with cream cheese frosting was always my favorite as a child, and I can't think of a better time than Valentine's Day to serve it. My cousin, Susan Tursi Tewksbury, gave me the recipe. She says it was inspired by the Waldorf Astoria Hotel's Red Cake. I think cupcakes are the perfect serving size. Using a cake mix makes this an easy dessert and it can be made ahead and frozen, too. This recipe makes 24, so there will be plenty for your guests to take home and for your children to enjoy, too.

1 box Pillsbury Moist Supreme German
    Chocolate Cake Mix
1 cup sour cream
½ cup water
¼ cup oil
1 (1 ounce) bottle red food coloring
3 eggs

Blend the cake mix, sour cream, water, oil, food coloring and eggs in a large bowl until well moistened. Beat with mixer on medium speed for two minutes. Pour the batter into paper lined muffin pans and bake at 350 degrees for 25 to 30 minutes. Cool, then frost.

– makes 24

frosting

¾ pound cream cheese, softened
½ pound butter, softened
1 pound confectioners' sugar, sifted
1 tablespoon milk
½ teaspoon vanilla extract

Blend cream cheese and butter together. Stir in confectioners' sugar, milk, and vanilla. Beat until smooth. When cupcakes are cooled, frost.

Wine Pairings

This menu calls for a big red wine such as a California Cabernet or a Brunello di Montalcino, both of which have sufficient tannins to stand up to the hearty beef and rich sauce. The 2007 vintage was wonderful for Napa Valley Cabernets. Good, medium-priced options include Franciscan and Clos du Val, and the Ladera "Napa" Cabernet would be a great choice for a bit more money.

While you can expect to pay a premium price for a Brunello, you'll be rewarded with a sublime experience. Fattoria dei Barbi and Col d'Orcia provide consistently good Brunello wines. But don't drink these wines too young. Ordinarily, you'll want to age a Brunello for at least seven years. (Seek out the 2001 and 2004 vintages.)

Carnivale

POLENTA WITH GOAT CHEESE AND SUN-DRIED TOMATOES

MUSHROOM AND CHEESE CRESPELLE

CHICKEN WITH PROSCIUTTO AND FONTINA

BROCCOLI WITH GARLIC

PIZZELLE WITH APRICOTS AND RASPBERRY SAUCE

Carnivale is a season of revelry that commences every year in Venice on the day after Epiphany (January 6). The pastry shops are full of rich delicacies, many of which are fried and contain a rich cream—and of course they're beautifully decorated. The season reaches a pitch of excitement during the eleven days prior to Ash Wednesday, with parades and costumed merry-making, and ends on *martedi grasso* (known as Mardi Gras or Fat Tuesday in other parts of the world). Everyone knows that Lent, a more austere season of fasting and reflection, lies just ahead.

In the Hobbins household, we do not celebrate this season with quite the gusto that the Venetians put into it, but on Fat Tuesday we often enjoy hosting a party along similar lines. You can throw your own Carnival celebration using these traditional and easy recipes. For example, I have included one dessert very similar to the rich pastries consumed in Venice during *Carnivale*—pizzelles with whipped cream, apricots with a raspberry sauce. I also include a rich and comforting winter dish—mushroom and cheese *crespelle* (an Italian crepe) that makes good use of the eggs, cheese, and milk we're less likely to consume during Lent. To heighten the festive mood, purchase colorful masks and beads for your guests to wear. Enjoy some music while you dine and a game or two if you're so inclined. You can make much of the food ahead, the better to join in the evening festivities yourself.

polenta with goat cheese and sun-dried tomatoes

Polenta is a staple food in the northern part of Italy and easy to make. My recipe suggests using the pre-made rolls you'll find on the grocery shelves, but it's quite easy to make your own polenta following the recipe on the package. Pour the warm polenta on a baking sheet that has been lined with foil and sprayed with Pam. Spread the polenta evenly and let cool. When it's firm, turn out the polenta on a board, and using cookie cutters, cut out the hearts and stars that will become the base for these antipasti. Then follow the recipe. You can make these delicious bites and freeze them up to a month ahead, baking them just before serving. Remember to take them out of the freezer about an hour before baking.

    6 ounces of goat cheese, crumbled
    3 tablespoons of milk or half and half
    12 slices of firm polenta cut about ½ inch thick
    Sun-dried tomatoes, drained
    1 tablespoon extra virgin olive oil

Preheat the oven to 350 degrees. In a bowl, combine the goat cheese and milk or half and half. When smooth put the mixture in a pastry bag fitted with a small star tip.

Cut the pre-made roll of polenta into 12 slices, or if you have made your own polenta, use a cookie cutter to cut the polenta into hearts or stars. If you don't have cookie cutters, cut the polenta into squares.

Top each piece of polenta with the goat cheese mixture and a strip of sun-dried tomato. Brush a cookie sheet with the extra virgin olive oil and place the polenta on top. Bake for 10 minutes or until the polenta is heated through.

– serves 8

crespelle

Crespelle are Italian pancakes or crepes. This traditional dish of Carnival is eaten in order to use up the eggs, cheese and milk in the house before the solemn season of Lent begins and rich foods are to be avoided. This recipe produces a light crespelle, suitable to use with other fillings at another time to make a very different meal. Serve this wonderful dish as a first course, while the chicken is baking in the oven.

batter

6 eggs
1 teaspoon salt
1 ½ cups water
1 ½ cups all-purpose flour
Canola oil to grease the griddle

In a mixing bowl add eggs, salt, and water, then gradually add flour and mix until smooth. Let the mixture rest in the refrigerator for 20 minutes. Stir again. Ladle out about ¼ cup of the batter into 4 inch circles on a hot, lightly oiled griddle and cook the first side until golden. Flip the crespelle over and cook the second side. Transfer to parchment paper.

filling

2 tablespoons unsalted butter
½ pound cremini mushrooms, stems
    trimmed and sliced
Salt and freshly ground pepper to taste
⅔ cup milk
10 ounces Fontina cheese, cut in small pieces
1 ounce Gorgonzola cheese, crumbled
2 egg yolks
¼ cup milk
¼ cup freshly grated Parmesan cheese

Melt the butter in a skillet over moderate heat and cook the mushrooms, seasoned with salt and pepper, about 5 minutes until softened. Set aside.

Heat the ⅔ cup milk in the top of a double boiler over simmering water. Blend the Fontina and Gorgonzola cheeses into the milk, stirring until they melt into a sauce. Beat the egg yolks in a bowl, and add ¼ cup of the warm cheese sauce, beating vigorously. Pour egg mixture back into the cheese sauce and cook, stirring constantly for 3 to 4 minutes. Remove from the heat.

Take ½ cup of the cheese sauce and combine it with the mushrooms. Combine the remaining ¼ cup milk into the reserved cheese sauce, and mix well.

Spread 1 tablespoon of the mushroom-cheese mixture on each crespelle and roll them up and place, seam side down, in a 9x13 inch- baking dish that has been sprayed with Pam.

Spoon the remaining cheese sauce over the crespelle and sprinkle with the Parmesan cheese. Bake in a preheated 450 degree oven for15 minutes, or until the top is browned.

– serves 8

chicken with prosciutto and fontina

I have been using the recipes from this menu in my cooking classes for years. This chicken is quite simple to prepare, and my clients have always loved it. Make sure to pound out the chicken breasts so that they are a bit thinner and easier to roll. It is important that the breasts have the skin on, as this keeps them nice and moist and gives the chicken so much color and flavor. If you do not want to bone the chicken yourself, ask your butcher to do it for you. You could close the rolls up using three toothpicks—the way my mother always does it. Before serving, remove the picks for a nicer presentation.

2 tablespoons extra virgin olive oil, plus extra
1 onion, diced
2 bay leaves
1 bunch of escarole, cleaned
8 boneless chicken breasts with skin
8 slices of Fontina cheese
8 thin slices of prosciutto
Salt
Freshly ground black pepper

Preheat oven to 350 degrees. In a large skillet over medium heat, warm the olive oil. Add the diced onion and bay leaves and sauté until the onion is translucent.

Roughly chop the escarole and add it to the skillet. Sauté until the escarole just begins to wilt and season it with salt and pepper. Remove the escarole from the heat and place it in a baking dish, which has been sprayed with Pam.

On a clean work surface, arrange the chicken skin side down. Cover the chicken with Saran wrap and pound with a meat mallet until flattened. Salt and pepper each chicken breast and place a slice of Fontina cheese on top. Add a slice of prosciutto on top of the cheese. Roll the chicken breast tightly and secure with toothpicks.

Place the chicken breast roll seam side down on the escarole in the baking dish. Drizzle with olive oil, and then sprinkle with salt and pepper to taste. Place the baking dish in the oven and bake for 40 minutes or until the juices run clear when a breast is pierced with a fork. Remove bay leaves before serving.

– makes 8

✦

CARMELA COMMENTS | These rolls could be made earlier in the day and held in the refrigerator until ready to bake. Set them on the counter for about an hour before baking to take the chill off.

broccoli with garlic

Broccoli is one vegetable that is always available and so good for you. I especially like this recipe because I spice it up with lots of fresh garlic and red peperoncino or red pepper flakes found at a good grocery store or spice shop. Make this dish while the chicken is baking in the oven and serve the chicken and broccoli together.

6 large garlic cloves
3 pounds of broccoli
¼ cup extra-virgin olive oil
Salt to taste
¼ teaspoon dried peperoncino (dried
    hot red pepper flakes)

Peel the garlic cloves and slice into pieces. Cut the broccoli into florets and cut the tender part of the stalk into pieces.

Pour the olive oil into a sauté pan and, when heated, add the garlic. Cook the garlic, stirring until lightly browned, taking special care not to let it burn.

Add the broccoli and peperoncino and stir, making sure that the broccoli is covered with the olive oil.

Pour ½ cup of water over the broccoli. Cover the pan and raise the heat slightly and cook the broccoli for an additional 5 minutes. Shake the pan occasionally. Remove the cover and toss everything again. Replace the cover and cook for another 5 minutes. Check for tenderness, cooking the broccoli longer if you want it softer. Remove the cover and serve.

– serves 8

pizzelles with apricots and raspberry sauce

*I*n *our Italian family, pizzelles are served at every holiday. For Christmas I make hundreds of them, sprinkled with confectioners' sugar and packaged for hostess gifts or for the church bake sale. While still warm, the pizzelles can be wrapped into a cone and later stuffed with pudding or whipped cream. They also can be molded around a custard cup and made into a bowl to use for an ice cream sundae, as I do in my "Kids in the Cucina" classes. I have jazzed up this recipe, which is typically served in Venice for Carnivale, and am using sweetened whipped cream, caramelized apricots and a raspberry puree for a very festive end to your Carnivale celebration.*

1 stick butter, melted and cooled
¾ cup granulated sugar
3 eggs
1 teaspoon pure vanilla extract
1¾ cup all purpose flour
2 teaspoons baking powder
Salt

Melt 1 stick of butter in the microwave oven or in a pot on the stove; remove it from the heat and let cool. When cooled, pour the butter into a mixing bowl, add the sugar and eggs and mix well. Add the vanilla extract and mix again.

In a separate bowl mix together the all purpose flour, baking powder and salt. Add the dry ingredients to the wet a little at a time until all of the flour mixture has been incorporated.

Heat the pizzelle iron until hot. Add 1 rounded tablespoon of batter to the iron and close the lid. Cook for a minute or until golden brown. Remove the pizzelle to parchment paper to cool and harden.

Repeat with the remaining batter. For this recipe, cut four of the pizzelles in half as soon as they come off the iron, while they're still warm. Reserve the halves to be used when assembling the dessert.

for the whipped cream

1 half pint of whipping cream
1 tablespoon confectioners' sugar
1 teaspoon pure vanilla extract

In a chilled bowl with chilled beaters, whip the cream slightly. Add the confectioners' sugar and vanilla extract and continue to beat until the cream is stiff. Chill until ready to use.

for the raspberry puree

1 (10 ounce) package of frozen raspberries
2 tablespoons of granulated sugar

Place the raspberries and sugar in a blender and puree until smooth. Add a bit of water if sauce is too thick. Pour the puree into a fine strainer, and push the sauce through into a bowl, removing the seeds from the sauce. Chill until ready to use.

for the apricots

¼ cup of unsalted butter
3 tablespoons of sugar
24 dried apricots

At serving time, melt the butter in a sauté pan. Add the sugar and apricots and cook until the sugar begins to caramelize. Remove from the heat.

assembly

Place one whole pizzelle on each of 8 dessert plates. Add a dollop of whipped cream to the top and insert one of the half pieces of pizzelle into the whipped cream. The whipped cream will allow the half to stand up on its own. Spoon 3 of the apricots and the sauce around the plate and drizzle the raspberry puree around and over the pizzelle in a decorative fashion.

– serves 8

✦

CARMELA COMMENTS | Store the pizzelles in a box lightly covered with waxed paper. They can be made up to a week ahead of time and kept in a cool dry place. After making the raspberry puree, I put it in a squeeze bottle so I can decorate the plates easily. This sauce is also good on ice cream.

Wine Pairings

While a chicken entré normally calls for a Chardonnay, this is a chicken dish with gusto supplied by the prosciutto and fontina cheese. Those elements of the dish suggest a red wine to us, and the fruit-forward blended red wines of the Valpolicella region near Verona, Italy are just the ticket! A perennial favorite of ours is Allegrini's "Palazzo della Torre." This wine is a blend of Corvina, Rondinello and Sangiovese grapes. Another great choice is the lighter-bodied Tomassi "Rafael" Valpolicella.

For a white wine pairing, a Chardonnay or a Sauvignon Blanc will have the body and acidity to match the flavors of these dishes. We discuss Chardonnays in some detail in the proposed pairings for "Dinner at the Latin King" a bit later in this book. For fans of Australian Chardonnay, the curiously-named "The Lackey" Chardonnay drinks nicely with this meal. The somewhat lighter Sauvignon Blanc wines we have most enjoyed with this menu are California's St. Supery and Australia's Villa Maria "Cellar Selection."

As one final indulgence, consider enjoying a glass of chilled Moscato d'Asti wine with this menu's delightful pizzele dessert. This sweet, slightly effervescent (or "frizzante") wine of Italy's Piedmont region will add a special touch. Castello del Poggio and Batasiolo are reliable labels to seek out.

Easter Lunch

ARTICHOKE BRUSCHETTA

FETTUCCINE WITH PEAS AND HAM

LEG OF LAMB STUFFED WITH SPINACH AND MUSHROOMS

MADEIRA SAUCE

SAGE-ROASTED POTATOES

SAUTEED GREEN BEANS

SPINACH SALAD WITH PARMESAN DRESSING

BERRIES ON A CLOUD

Easter may come in March or April, but usually signals the beginning of spring, following a long Lenten season when many of us have been fasting and abstaining. At this time a food celebration is in order, and I feel that this menu provides just that. The dishes I've selected include many different spring foods, from the artichoke bruschetta to the fresh berries in our dessert. Italians usually serve lamb as the main course, for its symbolism of Christ as the sacrificial lamb who saves us all. So, following tradition, lamb is the main course for this menu. A similar recipe for stuffing was given to me by my cooking teacher in Chianti.

I suggest that you serve this menu for Easter lunch as they do in Italy. A few years ago my family was able to spend Holy Week and Easter with family and friends in Rome. What a special time that was for all of us! After Mass at St. Peter's Basilica with Pope John Paul II, we walked to our friends' home for a wonderful Italian feast. After many courses, we concluded our meal by cracking open a huge chocolate Easter egg containing little gifts for all of us, and we toasted with a cool, crisp glass of sparkling Prosecco. This was followed by a nice *siesta* and then a long evening stroll—or *passaggiata,* as the Italians call it—through the beautiful ancient city. We treated ourselves with a gelato at the Piazza Navona as we chatted with other Italians and strolled home, having celebrated a most wonderful holiday. The Italians also celebrate Pasquetta or "little Easter" the next day. I suggest that you arrange to take Easter Monday off and have a picnic, visit a park, or just relax with your own family, extending this spring weekend as they do in Italy.

artichoke bruschetta

This bruschetta is easy to make, and everyone loves it. It seems that artichokes are always on an Easter menu in some form, and the combination of the artichokes and Romano cheese are perfect for this one.

1 (6½ ounce) jar of marinated artichoke
    hearts, drained and chopped
½ cup grated Romano cheese
⅓ cup finely chopped red onion
5 tablespoons mayonnaise
1 French baguette, cut into ⅓-inch slices
extra virgin olive oil
finely chopped parsley for garnish

Preheat the oven to 350 degrees. In a medium bowl, mix marinated artichoke hearts, cheese, red onion and mayonnaise. Brush the bottoms of the baguette slices with olive oil. Top the baguette slices with equal amounts of artichoke mixture. Arrange slices in a single layer on a baking sheet. Bake in the pre-heated oven for 10 minutes, or until the bruschetta is bubbly on top and lightly browned on the bottom. Sprinkle with finely chopped parsley.

– serves 8

fettuccine with peas and ham

This is a classic spring recipe from the area of Emilia-Romagna, where cream and butter are commonly used in pasta sauces. Fresh peas are best for this pasta dish, but frozen are perfectly acceptable and much easier. We are using this as a pasta course for this menu, but with a salad and another vegetable this pasta is a perfect main course.

2 tablespoons unsalted butter
2 tablespoons extra virgin olive oil
3 tablespoons onion, chopped
¼ cup cooked ham, diced in ¼ inch pieces
Salt and freshly ground black pepper to taste
¼ cup chicken stock
1 pound fresh green peas, shelled, or
    1 (10 ounce) package frozen peas, thawed
1 pound fettuccine
½ cup heavy cream
½ cup grated Parmesan cheese
¼ cup finely chopped parsley

Heat the butter and olive oil in a skillet over moderate heat. Add the chopped onion, and cook for 3 to 4 minutes or until the onion is soft.

Add the chopped ham, salt and pepper to the skillet. Cook for 2 minutes, while stirring. Add ¼ cup of the stock and the peas then simmer for 2 minutes.

Cook the fettuccine in a large pot of salted, boiling water until the pasta is *al dente*. Just before the fettuccine is done cooking, add the cream to the skillet of sauce and stir until heated through and well-blended.

Drain the fettuccine, and spread the pasta out on a flat platter or pasta dish. Pour the ham and pea sauce over it. Sprinkle with the Parmesan cheese and parsley and toss before serving.

– serves 8

✦

CARMELA COMMENTS | Cook your pasta in a large amount of rapidly boiling salted water. To cook it *al dente* means to cook it "to the tooth," or so that when you test it there is still some "bite" to the pasta.

Wine Pairings

This menu's featured dish of savory lamb presents the opportunity for numerous delightful pairings with hearty red wines. It would be hard to go wrong with a Cabernet Sauvignon, an Argentine Malbec, or even a Zinfandel. We suggest taking advantage of the powerfully-flavored Shiraz wines coming to us from Australia or one of the many quality Syrahs produced on our West Coast.

In selecting Australian Shiraz, look for wines originating in the McLaren Vale or the Barossa Valley. Peter Lehmann's "The Clancy's" Shiraz is deservedly quite popular and widely available. Another good Shiraz is Thorn-Clark's "Shotfire." For something special, try the colorfully-named "Two Left Feet" from Mollydooker, a blend of Shiraz, Cabernet, and Merlot. A very nice domestic option is the Elemental Cellars Syrah from Oregon's Willamette Valley (especially the 2006 vintage). Here again, the tannins in these wine require a bit of bottle age to ensure a peak drinking experience.

leg of lamb stuffed with spinach and mushrooms

Leg of lamb is always on the Easter table in Italy, and I usually serve it as well. I make the stuffing early in the morning or even the day before, and then assemble the dish when the stuffing has cooled. Use lots of rosemary and garlic, and make sure to pass some sauce or mint jelly to go along with the lamb.

stuffing

1 (10 ounce) package of chopped frozen
    spinach, thawed and squeezed dry
4 tablespoons extra virgin olive oil
1 cup onion, chopped
4 garlic cloves, minced
1 (8 ounce) package button mushrooms,
    finely chopped
Salt
Freshly ground pepper to taste

Thaw the spinach and squeeze it dry. Heat the extra virgin olive oil in a large skillet. When hot, add the chopped onion and minced garlic and cook until the onion is soft. Add the chopped mushrooms and cook until the mushrooms release their liquid. Add the spinach, stirring it into the mushroom and onion mixture. Add salt and pepper and cook until the mixture is dry. Set aside to cool.

assembling

1 (6-7 pound) boneless leg of lamb, trimmed
    and butterflied to 2 inch thickness
2 tablespoons extra virgin olive oil
1 tablespoon rosemary, chopped
1 tablespoon thyme, chopped
Salt and freshly ground black pepper
4 cloves garlic

Preheat oven to 425 degrees. Open butterflied lamb like a book and place it cut-side up on a work surface. Sprinkle with salt and pepper. Spread the spinach and mushroom mixture evenly over the lamb. Starting at the narrow end, roll up lamb tightly, enclosing the filling. Tie the lamb with kitchen string at 2-inch intervals to hold its rolled-up shape. Rub the outside of the lamb with olive oil, rosemary and thyme. Sprinkle with salt and pepper. Cut the cloves of garlic into slices. Using a small sharp knife, cut several 1-inch-deep slits in the lamb and insert the garlic slices into them. Place lamb on a rack in a roasting pan.

Roast lamb to desired doneness or until an instant-read thermometer inserted into the thickest part of lamb registers 135-140 degrees for medium rare. This should take about 1 hour and 25 minutes. Remove the lamb from the oven. Cover with foil and let stand for 15 minutes. Remove string and cut lamb into ½-inch-thick slices. Serve with Madeira sauce.

– serves 12

madeira sauce

T*his is a delicious sauce with lamb, but it's also excellent on beef. It could be made earlier and reheated when ready to serve. You may want to double the recipe so that you have extra sauce. That will allow you to make a Shepard's Pie with the leftovers from your Easter dinner.*

4 tablespoons butter
4 tablespoons flour
2 cups beef broth
¾ teaspoons ground thyme
2 sprigs fresh parsley
¾ cup good quality Madeira

In a saucepan, melt the butter over low heat. Blend in the flour and cook, stirring until smooth and bubbly. Slowly add the beef broth and stir. Add the thyme and parsley and heat to boiling, while continuing to stir. Boil for 1 minute and remove from the heat. Discard the parsley and add the Madeira. Return to the heat and simmer until thickened.

Serve over the lamb or pass the sauce at the table.

– makes 2 cups

sage-roasted potatoes

Easy to make, these potatoes are always requested by my family. I prefer to use small red potatoes.

2 pounds of potatoes, cut in wedges
1 tablespoon dried Italian herbs
Salt and freshly ground black pepper to taste
Extra virgin olive oil
6-8 fresh sage leaves, chopped

Wash potatoes and cut into wedges. Place them in a roasting pan in a single layer. Sprinkle the potatoes with the dried Italian herbs, salt and pepper and drizzle with olive oil. Toss the potatoes well, making sure each piece is well coated.

Place potatoes in the oven and roast at 350 degrees for 30 minutes. Remove potatoes from the oven, add the fresh sage to the potatoes, and toss. Then roast the potatoes for an additional 5 to 10 minutes or until they are nicely browned and can be easily pierced with a knife.

sauteed green beans

2 pounds fresh green beans, washed
    and ends trimmed
4 tablespoons extra virgin olive oil
2 cloves of garlic, chopped
1 teaspoon Italian seasoning
½ cup toasted pine nuts
Salt
Freshly ground black pepper

Plunge the green beans into a large pot of rapidly boiling salted water. Cook until tender but crisp—about 5 minutes. While the beans are cooking, prepare a large bowl of ice water. Drain the beans and immerse them in the ice-water bath. This process will stop the cooking, leaving your beans crisp and preserving their bright green color.

Toast the pine nuts in a dry sauté pan until lightly browned. Remove to a plate to cool until ready to serve

At serving time, heat the olive oil in a large skillet; when the oil is hot, add the garlic. Do not let the garlic burn. Add the cooked green beans and the Italian seasonings, then toss well. Add salt and pepper to taste and toss again, continue cooking until the beans are heated through. Garnish with the pine nuts.

– serves 8

parmesan dressing

This dressing can be made in a covered jar early in the day and refrigerated. If you do so, allow it to come to room temperature before serving the salad. Use the best quality olive oil available.

¾ cup extra virgin olive oil
¼ cup fresh squeezed lemon juice
2 tablespoons freshly grated Parmesan cheese
¾ teaspoon salt
Freshly ground pepper to taste
Dash paprika
1 clove garlic, halved

In a covered jar, combine all of the ingredients and shake until well blended. At serving time discard the garlic from the dressing and pour the dressing over the spinach leaves and onion rings. Toss well. Add additional freshly ground black pepper and extra grated Parmesan cheese.

– serves 8

spinach salad with parmesan dressing

Soaking the raw, sliced red onion in an ice water bath will take away the strong taste and keep the onion very crisp.

2 (10 ounce) bags of baby spinach
1 medium red onion, thinly sliced into rings

Wash and dry the spinach. Set aside in a large bowl and keep refrigerated until serving time.

Thinly slice the red onion and place the slices in a bowl of ice water. Set aside until serving time.

berries on a cloud

The recipe was given to me in 1974 at a bridal shower thrown for me by some friends just before I was married. Along with a gift each guest was asked to bring her favorite recipe to share with me so that I could begin my recipe collection. This was originally named "Forgotten Dessert" because you made the base of this recipe (the "cloud") at night just before going to bed. It was placed in a warm oven, and then the oven was turned off. When you got up the next morning, the egg whites had turned into a stiff meringue, a perfect base for the whipped cream and berries.

I made this dessert often as a young bride, but then I either forgot about it or lost the recipe. Recently, I was at a bridal shower for my daughter-in-law, Kate, and Berries on a Cloud was served. I asked the hostess, Julie McHugh, to share her version of the recipe with me, and she generously agreed. I think this dessert is the perfect finale for this springtime meal, and I hope you do too.

layer 1

6 egg whites at room temperature
½ teaspoon cream of tartar
¼ teaspoon salt
1½ cups granulated sugar

Combine egg whites, cream of tartar and salt, then beat until firm. Begin to slowly add the sugar and beat until the egg whites are stiff.

Preheat the oven to 275 degrees. Coat a 9x13 inch pan with cooking spray, and pour the meringue into the pan, making a bit of a depression in the middle of the pan. Place the pan in the oven and bake for 1 hour. Turn the oven off. Do not open the oven door, but leave the pan in over night.

layer 2

1 cup cold heavy whipping cream
1 tablespoon granulated sugar
1 teaspoon pure vanilla extract

Whip the cream in the bowl of an electric mixer fitted with a whisk attachment. When the cream starts to thicken, add the sugar and vanilla and continue to beat until firm, but do not over beat.

Spread the whipped cream over the first layer.

layer 3

½ pint fresh strawberries, hulled and sliced
½ pint fresh raspberries
½ pint fresh blueberries

In a bowl add all of the berries and toss with ½ cup of the cooled raspberry sauce. Pour the berries over the whipped cream and serve.

raspberry sauce

½ pint fresh raspberries
½ cup sugar
1 cup seedless raspberry jam
1 tablespoon Framboise liqueur

Place raspberries, sugar and ¼ cup water in a saucepan and bring the mixture to a boil. Simmer on low heat for 4 minutes and remove from the heat. Pour the raspberry mixture, the raspberry jam and the Framboise into a blender and process until smooth. Cool the sauce. Pass additional sauce at serving time.

– serves 8-10

Mother's Day Brunch

YOGURT AND GRANOLA SUNDAES

MINI-VEGETABLE FRITTATAS

ROASTED ITALIAN SAUSAGE

GRANDMA TURSI'S ZUCCHINI NUT BREAD

LITTLE FLOWER LODGE BLUEBERRY MUFFINS

CHOCOLATE-DIPPED STRAWBERRIES

Mother's Day arrives at an especially beautiful time of year. The trees are alive with blossoms, the tulips and other spring flowers are blooming, and the birds are singing. For my family, after a very long winter, this might be one of the first days we actually get to eat outdoors on our deck, signaling that spring has finally arrived and we have months of great weather ahead.

This brunch works wonderfully out-of-doors, but it can also be served in a more formal setting, with the children serving Mother in a beautifully set dining room, or on a tray in her bedroom while she has the morning to relax with her family. Just don't forget to clean up after brunch so that Mom really can enjoy her special day!

Most of this menu can be made ahead, with only the yogurt sundaes needing assembly while the frittatas bake and the sausage roasts. The muffins and bread can be made a day ahead (or even several weeks) and frozen. The chocolate-dipped fruit can be made a day ahead and kept fresh in the refrigerator, to be served on a beautiful silver platter the morning of your brunch.

These recipes can easily be adapted to feed the number you are serving. And with so many activities during May, such as First Communions and graduations, this menu provides a perfect way to entertain groups of people who may be coming at different times during the morning. No matter what the occasion, everyone is going to love these recipes.

homemade granola

This easy recipe makes a large quantity of granola, which you will want to enjoy with milk for breakfast, sprinkled over yogurt for a snack, with baked or fresh fruit, or just out of your hand. It's even great over ice cream. Yes, you can buy granola, but it's never quite as good as this. And you can change it up a little by using different nuts and dried fruits. With berries and yogurt, it combines into a tasty and healthy sundae for a spring brunch. It also makes a great gift.

Cooking spray, such as Pam
½ cup vegetable oil
½ cup pure maple syrup
1½ cups brown sugar
6 cups old-fashioned oatmeal
2 cups chopped pecans
1 cup wheat germ
1 cup sweetened shredded coconut
1 cup dried fruit, chopped
1 cup dried cranberries

Preheat the oven to 350 degrees. Spray two 11x17 inch jelly roll pans with cooking spray. In a microwave-safe bowl, combine oil, maple syrup, and brown sugar. Microwave this mixture on high for about 3 minutes or until the sugar begins to melt, being careful that it does not burn in the bowl or overflow. Remove from the microwave and whisk the mixture until it's well blended and there are no lumps.

In a very large bowl mix together the oatmeal, pecans, wheat germ and coconut. Toss well. Pour the syrup mixture over the oatmeal mixture and mix until everything is well combined. Divide the granola between the two baking pans and spread evenly.

Place each pan on an oven rack and bake for 10 minutes. Remove the granola from the oven and stir. Place the pans back in the oven, making sure you have rotated them. Bake an additional 10 minutes or until the granola is golden brown. Remove the pans from the oven and let them cool for 1 hour. Pour the granola back into a large bowl, add the dried fruit and cranberries, and mix well. Store the cooled granola in glass jars or canisters. It will remain fresh this way for up to 2 weeks.

– makes 14 cups

✦

CARMELA COMMENTS | Use only pure maple syrup, and don't use instant oatmeal, as it will burn. Wheat germ can be found in the supermarket near the cereal, and should be placed in the freezer once it is opened.

yogurt and granola sundaes

Granola sundaes look especially pretty in cut crystal glasses or bowls; even a wine glass makes a pretty presentation. You can make the sundaes a few hours ahead if you want, or just provide all of the ingredients and let your guests make their own. Portion size really depends on who is making them. This recipe provides the portions for a 1 serving sized sundae; you can make as many as you will need to serve your guests.

Granola
Yogurt, flavored or plain
Blueberries, raspberries, strawberries or
    other fresh fruit
Fresh mint

In a clear wine or parfait glass, place 1 tablespoon of granola, a layer of fresh fruit, and 2 tablespoons of yogurt. Repeat the layers. Garnish with a sprinkle of granola and top with a sprig of mint.

– makes 1 serving

◆

CARMELA COMMENTS | Any combination of fruit (fresh or frozen) will work, as will any kind of yogurt.

vegetable mini-frittatas

This delicious frittata can be made in a 9x13 inch pan, and when ready to serve it can be cut into squares. But for this Mother's Day brunch, I think making the small individual frittatas is a nice touch. If you want, you can switch the vegetables too, using red and yellow peppers or substituting green onions for the leeks. If there are any leftover frittatas, they can be warmed up in the microwave oven or even frozen for later use.

3 tablespoons butter
3 medium leeks
1 (9 ounce) carton of mushrooms
½ cup marinated sun-dried tomatoes
cooking spray, such as Pam
12 eggs
2 cups half and half
1 (8 ounce) package of Italian cheese blend, divided
1 ounce package of fresh basil, sliced into strips
½ cup finely chopped parsley
1 teaspoon salt
¼ teaspoon black pepper

Wash the leeks carefully, making sure that all sand and grit are completely removed. Dry the leeks and slice the white part only, then separate the slices into rings. Finely chop the mushrooms. With paper towels blot the sun-dried tomatoes to remove the oil and cut them into small pieces. Wash and dry the basil and parsley. Cut the basil into strips and chop the parsley.

In a large skillet, melt butter over medium-high heat. Add leeks and sauté until tender—about 5 minutes. Add mushrooms and cook for about 5 minutes or until soft. Stir in sun-dried tomatoes and cook until all of the vegetables are well blended.

Spray cupcake pans with cooking spray and evenly divide the vegetable mixture between the pans.

In a large bowl whisk together the eggs, half and half, 1½ cups of the cheese and the basil. Pour the egg mixture evenly over the vegetables. Bake the mini-frittatas in a 350 degree oven for 20 minutes or until a knife inserted in the center comes out clean. Top with the remaining cheese and return the frittatas to the oven until the cheese is melted. Remove them from the oven and let rest for a few minutes. Then sprinkle with the chopped parsley. When cool enough to handle, remove the frittatas from the pans, using a knife to loosen them from the sides of the pans.

– makes 24

◆

CARMELA COMMENTS | When cutting basil, I lay a large leaf on a cutting board and top it with several more leaves. I then tightly roll the leaves and cut the roll into strips. Shake the strips open and add to the egg mixture.

roasted italian sausage

One of my favorite memories of growing up was watching my two grandmothers make their own homemade sausage. They would use only the best quality pork and Italian spices. A trip to Graziano's Italian Market was necessary to purchase the pig intestines that provided casing for the sausage mixture. After washing the intestines and removing all of the salt in which they were packed, my grandmothers would thread the transparent intestine onto their meat funnel. Then the fun would begin as I watched the sausage take form. With their strong hands, my grandmothers would push the sausage mixture through the casing, twisting the casing every few inches to form links. This was a labor of love made for their families to enjoy between chunks of bread or in pasta sauces.

Today, when I'm visiting Des Moines, I always plan a stop at Graziano's, now my favorite Italian market. Established in 1912 by brothers Frank and Louis, the third generation of the Graziano family is now managing and operating this Des Moines landmark. The aromatic smell of Italian spices and herbs greets you the moment you step into the small, well-stocked grocery store. But it is the wonderful selection of meats, cheeses and pasta that always brings me back. And it would be unthinkable to leave the market without a good supply of their Italian sausage, which is made using the best quality pork and Italian spices, with no preservatives.

This recipe is simple and easy to make, so it is important to buy the best possible sausage, which you should be able to find in a good grocery store or specialty market. For lunch or dinner, I add sliced onions and peppers and roast them together with the sausage. I then put it all in a chewy Italian roll and am transported back to my childhood.

8 links sweet or spicy Italian sausage
Extra virgin olive oil

Brush links with olive oil and place in a heavy skillet. Roast in a 400 degree oven until sausages are cooked through and browned—usually about 15 minutes. Turn once.

– makes 8 servings

grandma tursi's zucchini bread

My Father, Joe Tursi, always had a huge garden that produced more zucchini than we could possibly consume. After my mother had stuffed, sautéed, fried and given away as much of the zucchini as she could, she would make loaf after loaf of this wonderful bread. She used the large zucchini that she said were more suitable for this recipe. I like to make several loaves of this moist, delicious bread at one time, and then wrap them well and freeze them for use whenever we need something a little sweet in the morning. They also make a nice quick hostess gift.

I like to bake this bread in 9x5-inch loaf pans. Use a serrated knife for slicing to insure a nice clean cut. I sometimes cut each slice in half and spread it with a thin layer of cream cheese or butter to create tea sandwiches.

2 cups shredded zucchini
3 eggs
1½ cups granulated sugar
1 cup canola oil
½ cup milk
1 teaspoon pure vanilla extract
3 cups flour
1 teaspoon cinnamon
1 teaspoon baking soda
1 teaspoon baking powder
½ teaspoon salt
1 cup chopped walnuts
Pam cooking spray

Shred the zucchini and set it aside. In a mixing bowl add the eggs and sugar and mix well. Add the canola oil, milk and vanilla extract and combine. Mix in the zucchini. In a separate bowl, combine the flour, cinnamon, baking soda, baking powder and salt. Gradually add these dry ingredients to the wet egg batter and mix. Gently fold in the chopped walnuts.

Spray two 9x5-inch loaf pans with cooking spray and pour the batter into the pans. Bake the loaves in a preheated 350 degree oven for about 50-60 minutes. Insert a wooden toothpick into the center of the bread; if it comes out clean, the bread is finished baking. It should be nicely browned on top and pulling away from the sides of the pan. Place on racks to cool. When completely cooled, remove from the pan and wrap each loaf in plastic wrap and foil to keep fresh.

– makes 2 loaves

✦

CARMELA COMMENTS | I don't peel the zucchini, as I like the green flecks in the bread and the extra fiber. You can make smaller loaves but it would be necessary to cut back the baking time. You could also turn this bread into muffins.

little flower lodge blueberry muffins

Our lake home, *Little Flower Lodge, on Big Sand Lake in the north woods of Wisconsin, is the perfect place for entertaining. We invite friends for the day and serve a big brunch before enjoying an afternoon of lake activities. Most weekends you'll find these muffins on the buffet table.*

During the summer months you can pick your own wild berries in northwest Wisconsin (if the bears haven't already found them). I also buy many pints of blueberries at the farm stands that pop up in the area to sell the local fruit, and freeze them on cookie sheets. Once they're frozen I put them in freezer bags so I have blueberries all year long for breads, muffins, pancakes and oatmeal.

¾ cup brown sugar
⅓ cup canola oil
1 egg
½ cup buttermilk
1 teaspoon pure vanilla extract
1½ cups flour
½ teaspoon salt
½ teaspoon baking powder
1 cup blueberries or other fruit
½ cup chopped nuts (optional)

In a large bowl mix the brown sugar, oil and egg, add the buttermilk and vanilla extract, and stir until blended. In another bowl mix together the flour, salt and baking powder. Gradually stir these dry ingredients into the wet mixture. When blended, fold in the blueberries and nuts. Pour batter into 12 paper-lined muffin pans and bake in a preheated 350 degree oven for 25-30 minutes. Insert a wooden skewer into the center of one of the muffins; when it comes out clean, remove the muffins from the oven and set on the counter to cool.

– makes 12 muffins

chocolate-dipped strawberries

This simple but delicious recipe can easily be made by the kids with adult supervision. I am suggesting strawberries, but other fruit can be used, such as pieces of banana or dried apricots. You can make this recipe a day ahead, but then they really need to be eaten. Do not use chocolate chips, as they do not melt well. This is a light dessert that makes an elegant end to any meal.

4 squares (1 ounce each) semi-sweet or
    bittersweet chocolate
1 tablespoon whipping cream
Dash of pure almond or vanilla extract
16 large strawberries

In a microwave-safe bowl, combine the chocolate and whipping cream. Microwave on medium heat for 30 seconds, remove and stir the chocolate. Repeat this every 30 seconds until the chocolate is completely melted. Stir in the extract and let the mixture cool for just a minute or two. Dip each piece of fruit into the warm chocolate and let the excess drip off. Place the strawberries on a waxed paper lined jelly roll pan. Refrigerate for about 15 minutes or until the chocolate is set. When ready to serve, place on a silver or white platter for a very pretty presentation.

– serves 8

Wine Pairings

A nice sparkling wine will provide a great accompaniment to this eclectic menu, with its combination of sweet and savory flavors. Though it would be hard to go wrong with a pricy French Champagne, Prosecco, the sparkling wine of Italy perfected in the Veneto, would also be an excellent choice, and most Proseccos are more affordable than their French counterparts. The Proseccos of Carpene Malvolti are among the best, though offerings from Zardetto and Col Vetoraz are also top-notch, and all three wines are widely available in the United States.

For an alternative from closer to home, consider the sparkling wines of California. Some of the larger French Champagne houses have established operations in the Napa and Anderson Valleys. French methods, including a second fermentation in the bottle, have likewise been more widely adopted there, resulting in substantially improved quality in the California offerings. Two favorites of ours are the Roederer "Anderson Estate" Brut and the excellent, food-friendly Blanc de Noir made by Schramsberg Vineyards of Napa Valley. Combining some orange juice with a Brut sparkling wine produces a great Mimosa—perfect for a brunch event.

Father's Day

CANNELLINI BEAN CROSTINI

CRAB SALAD MARTINI

LA SOSTANZA BISTECCA FIORENTINA

OR

CHICKEN IN BUTTER SAUCE

MARINATED SUMMER TOMATOES

CAPONATA

ORZO SALAD WITH ROSEMARY

RHUBARB CRISP

June can be such a busy time of year, with graduations, weddings, bridal showers, and other celebrations. Then there's Father's Day. My husband's birthday falls just a few days before Father's Day, so I'm usually guilty of lumping the two together into one special day for a wonderful guy. He doesn't mind, though, as I always gather our family and friends to help us celebrate with a great meal.

This menu is perfect for summer entertaining. I could not decide between two marvelous main courses, so I included both.

We first enjoyed these dishes at the well-known Florentine restaurant, Trattoria Sostanza. I was able to get a personal tutorial for making the chicken in butter sauce and also the recipe for the bistecca Fiorentina from the friendly chefs there. When you visit Florence, make sure to make La Sostanza one of your stops for a really great Tuscan meal.

The salads and crostini can be made ahead and assembled just before serving. Bob's favorite dessert, rhubarb crisp, can be assembled earlier and baked while you're eating the rest of your meal.

Pick and choose your favorite recipes from this meal for your own celebration, or make the entire menu and invite a whole gang over to honor your special father.

cannellini bean crostini

The people of Tuscany are known as mangiafa-gioli *or "bean eaters" because they love their beans with every meal. I just had to include a bean dish on this menu, as so many of the recipes used here are from Tuscany. I'm suggesting that you start your meal with this crostini, but if you want, keep the beans whole rather than mashing them and serve this as a side dish with either the beef or chicken. Tuscans would use dried beans and soak them overnight before cooking them. I simplify the recipe by using canned beans, which are a perfect substitute.*

1 (15 ounce) can of cannellini beans
1 tomato, seeded and diced
¼ cup red onion, finely chopped
2 tablespoons freshly chopped thyme or
    sage leaves
1 teaspoon lemon peel, grated
2 tablespoons freshly squeezed lemon juice
½ teaspoon kosher salt
Freshly ground black pepper
¼ cup olive oil
24 crostini

Rinse the beans in a colander and drain before mashing them to a chunky consistency. Dice the tomato and chop the onion and thyme or sage leaves. Mix with the lemon juice, grated peel, salt, pepper and olive oil. Toss everything together and refrigerate for several hours so the flavors can blend. At serving time, spread the tops of the crostini with the bean mixture and a grinding of black pepper. Garnish with some of the herbs and additional chopped tomato.

to make crostini

1 baguette
Extra virgin olive oil

Slice the baguette in ¼ inch slices. Brush both sides of bread with olive oil. Bake the crostini on a cookie sheet in a preheated 400 degree oven for about 5 minutes on each side. Remove from the oven. When cool enough to handle but still warm, rub a clove of fresh garlic over each side of the crostini.

– serves 8

crab salad martini

I lead yearly culinary tours to Savannah, Georgia. We have dear friends, John and Barbie Lientz, who have lived there for years, and we are usually lucky enough to spend some time with them when we visit. One spring evening, Barbie made a wonderful fresh crab salad for us. Because martinis are so popular now, I serve this salad as a first course in a martini glass, but any pretty container will work. It is so pretty, and everyone really appreci-

ates the extra touches that go into this dish. Thanks, Barbie, for sharing one of your favorite Savannah recipes. It has become one of my favorites too.

1 pound fresh lump crab
Zest of two lemons
Juice of 1 lemon
2 tablespoons capers
4 tablespoons chopped chives
1/3 cup mayonnaise
Salt
Pepper to taste

In a large bowl pick through the crab twice to make sure all shell pieces are removed. Add the lemon zest, juice, capers, chives and mayonnaise and mix well. Add salt and pepper to taste and mix again. Refrigerate until serving time.

assembly

8 martini glasses
Juice of 1 lemon
Old Bay Seasoning
16 asparagus tips, roasted
Extra virgin olive oil
Salt and pepper to taste
Boston lettuce leaves
Zest of 2 lemons
8 very thin slices of lemon
1 Roma tomato, chopped

Juice the lemon into a shallow bowl. Pour the Old Bay Seasoning mix into another shallow bowl and spread out. Dip a martini glass first into the lemon juice and then into the Old Bay Seasoning. Repeat with the remaining 7 glasses and let them dry while preparing the garnishes.

Lay the asparagus tips on a baking sheet. Drizzle with olive oil and sprinkle with salt and pepper. Roast in a 375 degree oven for 5-7 minutes, until they are tender but still crisp. Cool.

Chop the tomato. Zest two more lemons and set the zest aside. Cut the lemons in thin, cross section slices and then cut a slit in each slice, but do not cut all the way through.

Place a few lettuce leaves in the bottom of each of the 8 martini glasses. Scoop the crab salad evenly into the glasses. Garnish with 2 asparagus spears. Sprinkle a few pieces of chopped tomato over the top and complete the garnish with the lemon zest and a twist of sliced lemon.

– serves 8

✦

CARMELA COMMENTS | Shrimp or lobster could be substituted for the crab, or you could use a combination of the three.

bistecca fiorentina

My favorite Florentine restaurant is Trattoria Sostanza in the Santa Maria Novella neighborhood. Pasquale Compolmi opened this landmark restaurant in 1869 and it remained in the family until 1977. Now a new family is running the place but things remain much as they were when it opened. Open only during weekdays, two hours for lunch and two for dinner, you will get the best that Florence has to offer here. Tourists and locals alike line up early to get a table at this small, spare establishment, and the dining is communal. You might be sitting at a table with locals, tourists, or even a political figure. I have had great success going for lunch, but there have been nights when I have been turned away. So plan ahead if you want to include La Sostanza on your Florence itinerary.

La Sostanza is best known for their Bistecca (beefsteak) made from Chianina beef, served bloody rare. You won't find Chianina beef here, but a good porterhouse steak about 3 inches thick will work for this dish. Note that you may not like it quite as rare as the Italians do, so adjust the cooking time.

I suggest that you speak to your butcher about selecting a top-quality porterhouse steak for this dish. Cook the steak to the degree you like it, but please, please don't over-cook it or dry it out! After it has rested, allowing the juices to be redistributed throughout the meat, cut the meat from the bone and then into ½-inch slices. I like to finish the steak with a sprinkling of sea salt while it rests.

> 1 porterhouse steak, about 2½ to 3 inches
>   thick and about 3 pounds
> ½ cup extra virgin olive oil
> 3 tablespoons Italian sea salt
> Juice of 2 lemons
> 2 cloves garlic, minced

In a large glass pan, pour out the extra virgin olive oil; add the sea salt, juice of the lemons and minced garlic. Mix well. Add the steak to the marinade and cover all sides. Marinate for about 30 minutes to 1 hour at room temperature, turning the steak once.

Heat a gas grill on high heat. If using charcoal, make sure the coals are glowing but not still flaming. Having blotted off excess marinade, lay the steak on the grill and cook the first side 8 to 10 minutes. Turn the steak and cook an additional 8 to 10 minutes. Each time make sure that the steak is well browned and marked. With tongs, hold the steak on edge over the fire, cooking the edges for 2 to 3 minutes each. Total cooking time should be about 25-30 minutes. Check the steak with an instant read thermometer. It should read about 120 degrees for rare. Cook a few minutes longer if you want it more done. Sprinkle with additional sea salt and cover with foil. Let the steak rest about 10 minutes before slicing.

– serves 8

marinated summer tomatoes

Barbie Lientz introduced me to these wonderful marinated tomatoes. I like to serve them on a bed of field greens. You could serve them alone as well; just make sure that you have lots of crusty Italian bread to sop up all of those flavorful juices.

8 Roma tomatoes, cored and cut into wedges
3 tablespoons chopped fresh flat leaf parsley
2 tablespoons chopped fresh basil
2 tablespoons chopped fresh oregano
2 tablespoons chopped fresh thyme
2 cloves garlic, chopped
¾ cup extra virgin olive oil
¼ cup balsamic vinegar
1 teaspoon kosher salt
½ teaspoon freshly ground black pepper
Field greens (optional)

Core and cut the tomatoes into wedges, set aside in a bowl. Chop the herbs and garlic and add them to the tomatoes.

In another bowl add the extra virgin olive oil, balsamic vinegar and salt and pepper and mix very well until everything is well combined.

Pour the dressing over the tomatoes and toss well. Refrigerate for several hours or over night. Remove them from the refrigerator about an hour before serving to take off the chill. They may be served alone or you may pour them over a bed of field greens.

– serves 8

✦

CARMELA COMMENTS | The tomatoes in this recipe could be diced and added to crostini for an antipasti, or they could be sliced, drained of their liquid and added to a sandwich.

chicken in butter sauce

This may be the perfect La Sostanza recipe for those of you who don't eat beef. The chicken breast is bathed in the best quality butter, which seals in the juices. Considering that the recipe calls for a boneless, skinless breast, this chicken remains very moist, tender and juicy. Use the freshest chicken and butter you can find, as those really are the key ingredients for this dish. La Sostanza serves two breasts on a plate, with no garnish. I like to top the chicken breast when finished with a little lemon juice and some chopped flat leaf Italian parsley.

MY BROTHER AND sister-in-law, Bobby and Amy, and I were invited into Sostanza's small, crowded kitchen last year to watch the chef make our chicken.

We documented the cooking lesson with pictures and asked lots of questions. The secrets to this dish are using organic chicken breasts, the best quality butter (I use Kerry Gold), and then a small sauté pan to cook the breasts. I usually cook them two at a time and occasionally will use two small sauté pans at the same time. You can easily double this recipe.

> 4 single, skinless, boneless organic
>   chicken breasts
> 1 cup flour
> 1 teaspoon Lawry's Seasoning Salt
> ½ teaspoon freshly ground black pepper
> 2 well beaten eggs
> 1 stick best-quality butter and possibly more
> Juice of a lemon
> ¼ cup chopped flat leaf parsley

Put each breast in a zip lock bag or between two sheets of Saran wrap or parchment paper. With a meat mallet or your fist, pound the chicken breasts on a cutting board to flatten them out to about 1 inch thickness.

In a pie plate, add flour, Lawry's Seasoning Salt and ground black pepper, mixing well. In another pie plate, add two eggs to 1 tablespoon water and beat until well-combined and light.

Put two 8- or 9-inch sauté pans on lighted burners and melt the butter in them, using ½ stick in each pan. While butter is melting, dip the chicken breast first into the flour mixture and then into the egg mixture. Lay the coated chicken breast into the sizzling butter, placing top side down first.

Cook on the first side for 5 to 7 minutes, spooning the butter over the tops of the breast. Lightly salt and pepper. When the first side is nicely browned, turn the breast over and cook for an additional 5 minutes, all the while basting the top with the butter. Lightly salt and pepper again. If you need more butter to baste the chicken, add about a tablespoon at a time to the pan, let it melt, and continue basting.

When the chicken breast is completely browned and springs back to the touch, it's done. You can also pierce the breast to see if the juices run clear. Pour a tablespoon of lemon juice over the chicken. Baste those sizzling juices over the chicken as well. Top each breast with chopped flat leaf parsley.

– serves 4

Wine Pairings

The classically Tuscan dishes comprising the bulk of this menu virtually demand a sangiovese-based wine from Tuscany, at least for the steak option. This is the time for a Chianti Classico Riserva from Fontodi or Rocca della Macie, especially from the 2004 vintage. Another delightful choice would be Chianti's first cousin, Vino Nobile di Montepulciano. The Avignonesi estate makes a wonderful version. For the budget-minded, Monte Antico "Toscana"—a mouth-filling blend of Sangiovese, Merlot and Cabernet Sauvignon—would be a great alternative.

Should you choose the chicken entré, the Chianti Classico will still work very nicely. For a white wine option, consider a Soave Classico from the Veneto region of northeast Italy. While this suggestion amounts to heresy in Tuscany, it makes for a lovely pairing with this chicken dish. Among our favorites are Pieropan's "La Rocca" Soave Classico Superiore and Inama's Vigneto du Lot Soave Classico. These have sufficient body to complement the richness of the chicken dish and its companions on the menu.

caponata

Caponata is best made in the summer when the vegetables are in season. This recipe is great as a side dish or heaped on chewy Italian bread.

1 medium eggplant
2-4 plum or Roma style tomatoes
2 stalks celery, diced
6 tablespoons extra virgin olive oil
1 red onion, sliced
20 pitted green olives
1 tablespoon capers
2 tablespoons red wine vinegar
1 tablespoon sugar
Salt
Freshly ground black pepper to taste
Crusty Italian bread, cut into chunks

Peel eggplant and cut into ½-inch cross-sections, laying them on paper towels. Sprinkle the pieces with salt and let rest for 30 minutes. The bitter juices of the eggplant will rise to the top. Blot the tops of the eggplant and turn the pieces over. Salt and let rest another 30 minutes. Blot again and cut into bite-size pieces.

Plunge the tomatoes into boiling water briefly. Then remove skins, cut tomatoes into bite-sized pieces and set aside.

In a 12-inch sauté pan, warm 4 tablespoons of the olive oil. Add the eggplant and sauté until soft. Remove the pieces from the pan and set aside.

Add remaining oil to the pan and sauté the sliced onion. Add diced celery and cook until soft. Add tomato, olives and capers and let everything blend together for a few minutes. Return eggplant to the pan and add the vinegar and sugar. Stir well and let simmer 10-15 minutes.

Serve warm or cold, with crusty bread.

– serves 8

orzo salad

This pasta salad is a favorite of my son Brian and his wife Kate. They tell me they know it's really summer when I make it. Prepare it early in the day to let the flavors blend.

1 pound orzo pasta
1½ cups toasted pine nuts
1 cup Feta cheese with basil and sun-dried tomatoes
2 garlic cloves, minced
¼ cup fresh rosemary, minced
½ cup extra virgin olive oil
Zest of 1 lemon
Juice from 1 lemon
1 cup Niçoise olives
Fresh spinach or arugula (optional)

Cook orzo in boiling salted water. Taste often so that it is not over cooked. Drain the orzo and run it under cold water to stop the cooking.

In a sauté pan toast the pine nuts in a little extra virgin olive oil. Watch carefully so they do not burn. Set them aside to cool.

Place the pasta in a large bowl and crumble the Feta cheese over the cooled pasta.

In a jar add the minced garlic, fresh rosemary, extra virgin olive oil, together with the zest and juice of the lemon. Shake well, then pour over the pasta and mix. Add the pine nuts and olives and mix again. Refrigerate. At serving time if you want, you could add some fresh chopped spinach or arugula. Or garnish with more pine nuts and sprigs of rosemary.

– serves 8

rhubarb crisp

My husband, Bob, doesn't care for cakes, but he loves fruit pies, cobblers and crisps. Since we're celebrating his big day, this menu includes his favorite—rhubarb crisp. The addition of cardamom to the recipe brings a special taste to it. This dessert is best served warm; bake it while eating your meal. Then serve it up with some good vanilla ice cream or sweetened whipped cream.

topping

½ cup old-fashioned oatmeal
½ cup all purpose flour
½ cup (packed) golden brown sugar
⅓ cup chopped walnuts
¼ teaspoon freshly ground nutmeg
Pinch of salt
6 tablespoons chilled unsalted butter, cut into
    ½-inch cubes

Mix first 6 ingredients in the bowl of a food processor, pulsing 3-4 times. Add butter and continue pulsing until moist clumps form.

filling

7 cups fresh rhubarb, sliced ½-inch thick
¾ cup granulated sugar
⅓ cup orange juice
2 to 4 tablespoons all purpose flour, divided
1½ teaspoons grated orange peel
½ teaspoon ground cardamom
¼ teaspoon ground nutmeg

Preheat oven to 375 degrees. Butter a 9x13 inch pan. Begin by using only 2 tablespoons of flour, combining all of the filling ingredients in a large bowl and stir to blend. Let the mix rest until juices form; if there is too much juice, add remaining 2 tablespoons of flour and mix. Pour the filling into the prepared pan and spread evenly. Sprinkle the topping evenly over the filling. Bake until topping is golden brown and crisp and the filling is bubbling around the edges—about 45 minutes. Serve warm with ice cream or sweetened whipped cream.

COOL CUCUMBER MINT SOUP

MUSHROOM CROUSTADES

VEGETABLE SALAD ON A BED OF LETTUCE

SWORDFISH WITH PESTO SAUCE

PASTA VERDE

RASPBERRY AND GINGER SEMIFREDDO

I am lucky enough to be able to travel to Italy yearly. One of my favorite things to do while I'm there is to eat "al fresco" or outdoors, and we do this frequently. In the big cities, as well as small towns and villages throughout the country, you will find couples and families enjoying the cool summer breezes as they eat under the star-filled sky. Living in the upper Midwest, my opportunities to eat outside are limited, so I take advantage of them every time I can.

Dinner Al Fresco is a complete dinner menu that provides the perfect meal to share with family and friends while enjoying gorgeous summer evenings. This dinner can be prepared early in the day with the exception of the pasta (which takes only minutes to make) so the hosts can enjoy their party too. This lovely meal is perfect for a small birthday celebration or, if doubled or tripled, would be nice for a small bridal shower or engagement dinner. If you're entertaining a smaller group, the recipe amounts could be divided in half to serve just a few.

Find a protected spot in your garden or near the lake to dine and set the table with beautiful linens, china, and crystal. Then decorate with summer flowers and don't forget lots of candles to add a bit of romance to the evening. With Vivaldi playing in the background, you will have the perfect summer dining experience.

cool cucumber mint soup

*S*erve this pretty cold soup as a separate course in a soup bowl to be eaten with a spoon, or in a clear glass cup to be sipped. It needs to be made several hours in advance so all the flavors can blend together. At serving time all you will have to do is ladle it up and garnish it with a slice of cucumber and freshly-cut mint from your summer garden.

5 cucumbers
1½ cups plain yogurt
1 cup light sour cream
1 teaspoon English-style dried mustard
Salt and pepper to taste
½ cup chopped mint leaves
Mint sprigs for garnish

Peel and chop 4 cucumbers, reserving the last cucumber for garnish. In a blender or food processor, puree chopped cucumbers, yogurt, sour cream, mustard, salt, and pepper. Transfer to a bowl. Chill soup overnight or for at least 6 hours. Stir in chopped mint. When ready to serve, ladle soup into a small pretty bowl or cup and garnish the top with a thin slice or two of cucumber and a sprig of mint.

– serves 8

mushroom croustades

Mushroom Croustades are easy to make. In this recipe I have you spooning the mushroom mixture over the bread and then serving the croustades. An alternate would be to put the mushroom mixture in a pretty bowl, surround the bowl with crostini, and let everyone help themselves. You may be tempted to omit the anchovies in this recipe, but do not. The anchovies will melt into the mixture and you won't notice them, but they impart such a nice flavor to the mushrooms.

> 3 tablespoons extra virgin olive oil, plus extra for the bread
> 3 cloves garlic, mince 2, reserve 1 to brush on the toasted bread
> 1 pound of Baby Bella mushrooms cleaned, trimmed and sliced
> 3 anchovy fillets, chopped
> Salt to taste
> Freshly ground pepper
> Juice of one lemon
> 8 slices of country style bread, toasted
> ¼ cup freshly grated Parmesan cheese

In a nonstick pan, warm the olive oil over medium-high heat. Add the garlic and mushrooms and sauté for 5 minutes, stirring often. Add the chopped anchovy fillets, salt, pepper, and lemon juice and cook and additional 5 minutes or until the mushrooms are soft. Meanwhile, cut the bread into ¼- to ½-inch-thick slices, brush with olive oil, and toast in a 400-degree oven until lightly browned. When cool enough to handle, rub the pieces of toasted bread with a garlic clove. Spoon the mushroom mixture over the bread and sprinkle the Parmesan cheese over the top. Arrange on a beautiful platter and serve.

– serves 8

Wine Pairings

This wonderful summer meal calls for a white wine with body and just a touch of roundness to soften its acidity. A California Chardonnay will do nicely—Acacia's oaky "Carneros" is among our favorites. Other options include Frei Brothers' Russian River Chardonnay and the La Crema offering. For those who appreciate chardonnay in the French style, a white Burgundy would be a great choice. Try a Vincent Girardin Pouilly-Fuisse or the Domaine Manciat Macon-Charnay. But be careful not to serve these wines so heavily chilled that their richness is lost on the tongue.

If you're in the "red wine only" camp, think Oregon Pinot Noir for this meal. You'll be delighted. (See the Thanksgiving menu for a more detailed discussion of Pinot Noir.)

vegetable salad on a bed of boston lettuce

*M*ake *this colorful salad early in the day or even the day before serving and let the flavors blend. While cauliflower, broccoli, and carrots are the main vegetables in this salad, you could also add cherry tomatoes, sliced mushrooms, sliced red, yellow or orange peppers, or steamed green beans.*

1 head cauliflower, broken into small florets
1 bunch broccoli (about 1 pound) cut into
    bite-size pieces
8 carrots, peeled and cut into ¼-inch coins
1 head Boston lettuce

Drop cauliflower, broccoli, and carrots into boiling water for about 2 minutes. Meanwhile, prepare an ice-water bath. Remove the vegetables from the boiling water and plunge them into the ice water to stop the cooking and to set their bright color. The vegetables should be tender crisp. Remove vegetables from the ice water bath when they're cool and drain well.

vinaigrette

1 clove garlic, pressed or finely minced
Handful of fresh herbs such as parsley,
    thyme and chives, minced
1 tablespoon fresh lemon juice
1 tablespoon wine vinegar
½ teaspoon dry mustard
⅔ cup extra virgin olive oil
Salt and freshly ground pepper to taste

To make vinaigrette, shake all ingredients together in a cruet or glass jar. Pour vinaigrette over vegetables and toss together, making sure that the vegetables are well coated. Chill overnight in a big plastic container. Toss occasionally to mix everything together. When ready to serve, turn vegetables out on a lettuce-lined platter or arrange on individual salad plates.

– serves 8

✦

CARMELA COMMENTS | Use a very large pot to blanch the vegetables.

swordfish with pesto sauce

While visiting the Cinque Terre *along the Ligurian coast of Italy during our culinary tours, we have lunch at a restaurant called Bel Forte. We dine on their patio, which clings to the rocky shoreline. Our group is served the most wonderful seafood lunch, and of course there is pasta that includes pesto. This region of Italy is well known for both its excellent and abundant seafood and for its creamy* pesto. *We begin our meal with a pesto and pasta dish and then move on to seafood pasta tossed with many delicious crustaceans. Platters of grilled and fried seafood are then brought to the table and we all dig in for an amazing lunch. Swordfish is among the grilled fish we enjoy at that memorable meal and the inspiration for the following recipe.*

8 swordfish steaks, about 4 ounces each
4 teaspoons extra virgin olive oil
4 teaspoons freshly squeezed lemon juice
2 cloves of garlic, minced
¼ teaspoons salt
Pinch of freshly ground black pepper
Pesto sauce (page 92)

Combine olive oil, lemon juice, garlic, salt, and black pepper in a bowl. Brush the mixture on the fish and let it set for about 10 minutes. To broil, spray the rack of the broiler pan with Pam or olive oil and arrange the fish on the rack. Broil the fish 4 inches from the heat for 4-6 minutes per ½ inch thickness. If the fish is more than 1 inch thick turn it over half way through broiling. You can also grill the fish over very hot coals. Serve with pesto sauce.

– serves 8

✦

CARMELA COMMENTS | Other fish or seafood could be used for this dish such as tuna, salmon, or shrimp.

pasta verde

You will never make an easier pasta than this. That's why it's necessary to use the freshest ingredients you can find. For the spinach pasta look in your dairy case or go to an Italian specialty store. And while you're there, buy the best imported Parmesan cheese you can find. The final step to this pasta is to give each serving a topping of freshly ground black pepper and pass around more cheese.

> 1½ pounds spinach pasta
> ½ to ¾ cup butter
> ¾ cup freshly grated Parmesan cheese
> Freshly ground black pepper

Cook pasta in boiling salted water until *al dente*. While pasta is cooking, melt butter in a large skillet. When pasta is done, drain it well and transfer it to the skillet with the butter and toss to coat the pasta completely. Remove the pan from the burner, add the cheese and toss again and grind black pepper over the top. At serving time pass around extra grated cheese and the pepper mill.

– serves 8

✦

CARMELA COMMENTS | If you can't find fresh spinach pasta use the same quantity of a tri-colored dry pasta.

raspberry and ginger semifreddo

In Italian "semifreddo" means "half frozen." This summery dessert is much like ice cream, but soft and creamy, allowing the taste of fresh raspberries and ginger to really come out. It's a perfect end to a summer day, and the sauce provides me with my daily fix of chocolate. This dessert can be poured into a 9x5-inch loaf pan and sliced when you're ready to serve, or into cupcake pans or custard cups and unmolded before serving.

> 1 large ginger root, peeled and grated
> 1 cup fresh raspberries, plus extra
>   for garnish
> 1¼ cups of confectioners' sugar, divided,
>   plus extra for decorating dessert
> 2 cups heavy whipping cream
> 6 egg yolks
> Good quality pre-made chocolate sauce
>   or hot fudge sauce
> Fresh mint leaves

Place grated ginger into cheesecloth. Squeeze the cloth and strain the juice into a small pot over medium heat. Add the raspberries and ¾ cup of the confectioners' sugar, and bring to a boil. Stir often and cook until the raspberries are softened and the

sauce is syrupy—about 6 minutes. Remove from the heat and set aside to cool. In a bowl whip the heavy cream to medium peaks and set aside. In a separate bowl beat the egg yolks and remaining ½ cup sugar until frothy. Fold the egg mixture into the whipped cream and then gently add the raspberry syrup. Pour into a 9x5-inch loaf pan that has been lined with aluminum foil, making sure the foil overlaps the sides so you can easily remove the semifreddo. Freeze for 6 hours or overnight. At serving time cut the semifreddo into slices. Drizzle the semifreddo with chocolate and garnish with raspberries and a mint leaf, then dust the plate with some confectioners' sugar.

✦

CARMELA COMMENTS | Strawberries or a combination of berries could be substituted for the raspberries. When grating the ginger, I like to use a micro-plane.

Fourth of July

ANTIPASTI SKEWERS
FRIED GREEN TOMATOES ON BIBB LETTUCE
with MUSTARD DRESSING
SHRIMP BOIL
RED, WHITE AND BLUE
LEMON CURD TART

The Fourth of July is a uniquely American holiday that everyone loves to celebrate. When I was growing up in Des Moines, Iowa, my father was always given the job of going to McRae Park early in the day to reserve tables for the many families who would gather later for a huge potluck lunch of Italian specialties. Even though this is an American holiday, pasta, meatballs and sausage dishes were included with the fried chicken, potato salad, brownies and watermelon.

After lunch there were always games, the men playing bocce ball or a hand of cards while the children engaged in three-legged races and other games and competitions. This was the time when the women finally had a chance to relax and catch-up on the neighborhood gossip.

Many of the men were members of the American Legion, having faithfully served their country during World War II. The American Legion was then a very active group in Des Moines. One of the many events they sponsored was the annual fireworks display at Sec Taylor Stadium. While Dad and the other Legionnaires sold tickets, Mom and my brothers and I were in the stands watching local performers entertain until it was dark enough to begin the fireworks—the highlight of the day. Life could not get any better than this: sitting in the bleachers of our local baseball stadium on a hot July night, eating a snow cone and anticipating that first thunderous clap, signaling the beginning of the display that would light up the dark summer sky. Having completed his duties, Dad would slip into his seat next to my mother, and we would all watch the annual tribute marking our nation's birthday.

Today, I celebrate this favorite summer holiday at my home on Big Sand Lake with my own family.

We invite my three grown sons and their families, as well as our lakeside neighbors and any friends who might want to join us for the day. We begin our holiday by going to town to watch the local parade. Returning to the lake in the early afternoon, we enjoy a dip in the water or go for a pontoon boat ride, sometimes even participating in the colorful "boat parade" on our lake. After sharing this holiday dinner, we gather our flashlights, insect repellent and an extra libation before boarding the pontoon. As we drift out onto the quiet late, around us we see bonfires and flares on the shore. Soon the sky lights up just above the trees as the various nearby communities begin their annual ritual of fireworks displays in celebration of our nation's birthday.

antipasti skewers

By this time of year the farmer's markets, roadside stands and your own garden should be producing ripe cherry tomatoes and fragrant sweet basil. My cousin, Susan Tursi Tewksbury, first brought these antipasti to our home for a party, and this recipe has become one of our summer favorites. The skewers can be made early in the day and left to marinate while you take in the Fourth of July festivities or relax with a novel in a deck chair on the dock. These treats are easy to transport, so make a perfect antipasti to take along on a long afternoon boat ride. Everyone loves these skewers, so plan on at least 2 per person. After all that fresh air and summer fun, your guests will be hungry.

> 1 pound package of fresh tri-colored tortellini
> 1 pint grape tomatoes
> 1 bunch of fresh basil
> 1 can quartered artichoke hearts
> 1 pint fresh bococini mozzarella balls
> 1 pint pitted olives
> ½ pound salami, sliced thin
> 2 envelopes of Good Seasons Zesty Italian
>   Salad Dressing mix
> Bamboo skewers

Boil the tortellini for about 6 minutes in salted water. Drain and put the tortellini into a bowl of ice water to stop the cooking. Wash the tomatoes and basil and pat dry. Thread the tortellini, tomatoes, basil leaves, artichoke hearts, mozzarella, olives and salami (folded into quarters) onto the skewers. Using one package of the Italian salad dressing mix, make up the dressing by following the directions on the package, and drizzle the dressing over the prepared skewers. Sprinkle the contents of the second envelope of dry Italian dressing mix over the skewers and marinate for several hours. Assembled skewers can be stuck into a melon or pineapple half, or laid on a lettuce-lined tray.

– serves 8

fried green tomatoes on bibb lettuce with mustard dressing

I lead yearly culinary tours to Savannah, Georgia. Fried green tomatoes are very popular in the south and are often part of the excellent cooking classes we enjoy while touring the area. They combine perfectly with Bibb lettuce and a creamy mustard dressing—a real southern treat to accompany our shrimp boil. You may have to ask the produce manager at your grocery store to order the green tomatoes for you or check out local farmers' markets for them. So put a little "South" in your mouth, and treat your guests to this special dish.

fried green tomatoes

¼ cup buttermilk
¼ cup milk
1 egg
½ cup cornmeal
¼ cup all-purpose flour
1 teaspoon salt
½ teaspoon fresh ground black pepper
¼ teaspoon cayenne pepper
4 green tomatoes, sliced ¼-inch thick
1 cup peanut oil for frying

In a bowl combine buttermilk, milk and egg. Mix well. In a separate bowl stir together cornmeal, flour, salt, black and cayenne peppers. Dip tomato slices in milk and egg mixture, and then dredge them in the cornmeal and flour mixture. Coat well. Heat oil in a skillet over medium high heat and cook tomato slices 2 to 3 minutes on each side until golden brown. Drain on paper towels.

dressing

2 tablespoons white wine vinegar
2 tablespoons prepared Dijon mustard
Pinch of dried tarragon, or a handful of
    chopped fresh tarragon
Salt to taste
Freshly ground black pepper
⅔ cup salad oil

In a small bowl mix together the vinegar, mustard, tarragon, salt and pepper. Slowly add the oil a bit at a time and whisk until the dressing is well blended and emulsified. Refrigerate until serving time.

Lay 2 or 3 large Bibb lettuce leaves on 8 chilled plates. Arrange 2 fried tomatoes on top of the lettuce leaves and drizzle with the dressing. Top with more freshly ground black pepper.

– serves 8

shrimp boil

I don't know about you, but by this time of the summer I'm growing tired of the burgers, brats, and hot dogs served at summer outings. I like to serve this shrimp boil because it's quick and easy, and everyone enjoys it. Our daughter-in-law Jeannie loves corn on the cob, and our son Patrick is crazy about shrimp, so this is a perfect meal to serve to them when they come for their summer visit. There is something included in the pot that everyone would want to eat. If we're eating out doors, I simply pour the drained shrimp boil onto a disposable plastic tablecloth or newspaper down the center of the table. When you're done eating, all you have to do is roll up the cloth or paper and throw it out—no dishes to clean up, and more time for summer fun. If we're eating indoors, I dish up this recipe onto large platters and put them on the center of the table. Our guests then just help themselves. Make sure to have plenty of clarified butter and cocktail sauce in bowls for everyone to dip into. And if you're serving this dish on a cool day, the shrimp broth can be ladled into cups and sipped to warm everyone up.

Old Bay's Seasoning Bag for Shrimp or
   Crab Boil
6 lemons, 3 sliced and 3 cut into wedges
3 small, new red potatoes per person

½ pound Kielbasa per person, cut
   into bite-sized chunks
2 small frozen onions per person
1 ear of corn on the cob (broken in half)
   per person
½ pound shelled, raw shrimp per person
½ to 1 pound snow peas, trimmed

In a lobster pot or other large pot, boil water with the bag of Old Bay Seasonings and the sliced lemons for 10 minutes. Add potatoes and cook for 10 minutes. Add Kielbasa and onions. Bring the pot back to a boil. When the potatoes are tender, add the corn. Bring the pot back to a boil and add the shrimp, cooking just a few minutes until shrimp are plump and pink. Add the snow peas and cook for just a minute. Drain the shrimp boil and either dump it onto a disposable tablecloth or dish it up onto platters. Drizzle with a squirt of fresh lemon juice before serving. Have extra lemons available for everyone to add more if they like.

– serves 8

◆

CARMELA COMMENTS | A few family-members can't eat shrimp, so I make them a separate pot for dinner. I omit the shrimp and also the Old Bays Seasoning mix, using just salt and pepper. Everything else should be safe for them to eat as long as you've kept it separate from the shrimp.

red, white, and blue lemon curd tart

Lemons grow abundantly in the Cinque Terre and along the Amalfi Coast of Italy. There are many wonderful lemon desserts that come from these areas. Nothing says summer like this tart, made with a short bread crust, lemon curd, whipped cream and fresh berries. My recipe calls for lemon curd that you can purchase at any good grocery store or specialty shop, but you could make your own curd if you wish. Use only the freshest blueberries and raspberries—or even home grown strawberries. At serving time cut the tart into wedges and place a slice on a pretty plate, decorating with a thin slice of lemon and more berries. And if it is perfection you are going for, serve a small glass of icy Limoncello liqueur with dessert.

1½ sticks butter
⅓ cup granulated sugar
½ teaspoon almond extract
1½ cups all purpose flour
1 cup lemon curd
½ pint fresh blueberries
½ pint fresh raspberries
½ pint whipping cream, whipped
2 tablespoons confectioners' sugar
1 teaspoon pure vanilla extract
Thinly sliced lemons for garnish
Extra berries for garnish

In an electric mixer, beat butter and sugar together for 4 or 5 minutes, or until pale and fluffy. Reduce speed to low and add almond extract, followed by flour. Mix until combined. Press dough into a round 10-inch tart pan with a removable bottom. Chill until firm, about 30 minutes. Preheat oven to 350 degrees. Remove tart pan from the refrigerator and bake the tart in the middle of the lower oven rack until the crust is golden—about 30-40 minutes. Cool on a rack.

When the tart is completely cooled, whip the cream with the confectioners' sugar and vanilla extract until soft peaks form, and then set aside. Spread the lemon curd evenly over the crust. Dollop the whipped cream over the lemon curd and spread evenly over the tart. Gently rinse the berries, pat dry and arrange them decoratively over the whipped cream. Refrigerate. At serving time, remove the sides of the tart pan. Slice the tart into wedges and decorate with a twist of thinly sliced lemon and more berries.

– serves 12

✦

CARMELA COMMENTS | Lime curd could be substituted for the lemon curd.

Wine Pairings

With the abundance of flavors showcased in this menu, there are many possibilities for good pairings, and summertime demands consideration of a good cold beer as one of them. The explosion of craft brewing throughout the country has brought the possibilities for pairing beer with good food to an entirely new level. A nice Belgian-style beer would be a great choice for this meal. It would be hard to go wrong with Chimay Red or with New Belgium Brewery's Trippel, Belgian-style golden ale made with a hint of coriander.

We also enjoy a nicely chilled dry rosé with this meal. This is not to be confused with the syrupy sweet rosés of our youth (remember Mateus?) or, God forbid, with "white zinfandel." There are much drier rosés, derived from heartier red varietals, which complement the savory flavors in this dish rather than competing with them. Ciro Rosato, made by Librandi Winery along the coast of Calabria in southern Italy, is a perfect expression of this style of wine. Other good choices include Raptor Ridge "Rose of Pinot Noir" from Oregon's Willamette Valley or Crios "Rose of Malbec" from the Mendoza region of Argentina.

CROSTINI OF SWEET BELL PEPPERS
GRILLED SALMON SALAD
HERBED POTATO SALAD
TORTELLINI SALAD IN PESTO
LEMON AND POLENTA CAKE WITH FRESH BERRIES

This lovely menu can be enjoyed with family and friends on a warm summer day in the garden, near a lake, on a boat or in a park. Everything can be made ahead and transported to wherever you choose to dine. It is perfect for a small bridal shower, Sunday lunch at your weekend home, a birthday party or any summer celebration.

Much of this menu comes from deep in the heart of Tuscany in Italy, where I bring my clients for cooking tours. The hilltop village of Tofori overlooking the city of Lucca is where my business partners, Doug Haynes and Doris Fortino, live and host our week-long culinary tours. We begin our trip with what we call our *Benvenuti Pranzo* or Welcome Lunch in their beautiful garden along the stream that runs beneath their home, *Il Mulino*. While our guests are getting to know each other, Doris and her assistant Daniela are busy in the cucina preparing the crostini of sweet bell peppers, the herbed potato salad, and the lemon and polenta cake with fresh berries.

Meanwhile, Doug and I welcome our guests with a chilled glass of Prosecco, and we all begin to relax, knowing that this is going to be a great week of fine wine, good food, and exciting sight-seeing.

One of our stops is the *Cinque Terre* on the beautiful Ligurian Sea. As we hike and ferry between the five fishing villages, we see and smell the basil that grows abundantly in that area. The *Cinque Terre* is famous for its basil, and that provides the principal ingredient for a delicious pesto sauce and the inspiration for my Tortellini Salad in Pesto.

Grilled Salmon Salad is really a merger of several different recipes I have put together to create one great main-dish salad. Served as part of this menu or on its own, it's sure to become a family favorite of yours.

Back in Tofori, our clients rise from the table after a long lunch, refreshed, relaxed and ready for their cooking week. After enjoying this summer meal, your guests will likewise feel as though they have been on a culinary adventure and will remember this experience for a very long time as well.

crostini of sweet bell peppers

Roasting the peppers under the broiler intensifies the flavors and adds smokiness to them. It also softens the flesh of the peppers so when they have been sealed in a bowl for a few minutes, you will be able to remove the skin easily. This is a colorful and tasty appetizer everyone is sure to enjoy.

3 large bell peppers, red, yellow, orange
  (or any combination of the 3)
10 slices crusty Italian bread
3 cloves garlic
½ cup olive oil (and a bit more to brush
  on the bread)
Salt and pepper to taste

Cut bell peppers in half, place on a grill pan and roast under the broiler for about 5 minutes, or until the skin on all sides is blackened. Remove the peppers from the pan and place them in a bowl. Cover the bowl so that they steam, loosening the skin. When the peppers are cool enough to handle, remove the skin and cut peppers into strips.

Meanwhile, cut the bread into slices and brush with olive oil. Toast the bread in a panini press or on a grill pan under the broiler until both sides are lightly browned. While still warm but cool enough to handle, rub each piece of bread with a clove of garlic.

In a sauté pan add the remaining olive oil and 2 finely chopped cloves of garlic. Cook over medium heat until garlic softens, being careful not to let it burn. Add the sliced pepper strips, salt and pepper to taste and cook for about 2 minutes or until the peppers are warmed through. Top the bread slices with the sautéed pepper strips and add more freshly ground pepper to the tops of the crostini. Serve while warm.

– serves 10

herbed potato salad

Summer is the perfect time for this simple potato salad. It requires so few ingredients that each must be as fresh and perfect as possible. Don't even think about using yesterday's left over potatoes! The potatoes cooked in their jackets must still be warm when you add the herbed Italian dressing so that it soaks into them, making for a very flavorful salad.

5 pounds small new potatoes, quartered
2 cups herbed Italian dressing.

Add potatoes to a pot and cover with water by 1 inch. Add 2 teaspoons of salt and bring to a boil. Cook potatoes until fork tender—about 20 minutes. Drain potatoes. While they are still warm but cool enough to handle, pour the herbed Italian dressing over the potatoes and gently toss, making sure each piece is well coated.

herbed italian dressing

½ teaspoon salt
¼ teaspoon freshly ground black pepper
2 teaspoons each of fresh Italian parsley, rosemary, thyme, oregano and basil, all chopped fine
1 cup best quality extra virgin olive oil

Place all of the above ingredients in a jar. Shake or whisk the ingredients until they are well blended. Pour dressing slowly over the warm potatoes and stir gently. Serve warm or at room temperature.

– serves 8

grilled salmon salad

Grilled Salmon is one of my family's favorites. I add field greens, boiled eggs, crisp green beans, cherry tomatoes and olives to this salad and garnish it with pine nuts and Parmesan cheese. Tossed with a light vinaigrette, this salad could be the main dish or part of a salad buffet. Because most of it can be made ahead, the last-minute assembly is quick and will not take you away from your guests for too long. Make sure you buy the freshest salmon available and purchase fresh garden produce for this delicious salad.

2 pounds of fresh salmon fillet, cut into
    8 equal pieces
4 tablespoons extra virgin olive oil
4 tablespoons freshly squeezed lemon juice
1 teaspoon salt
½ teaspoon freshly ground pepper
2 teaspoons dried dill weed

Mix the olive oil, lemon juice, salt, pepper and dill weed together in a 9x13-inch glass pan. Add the pieces of salmon, coating both sides well, and marinate for 20 minutes. Remove the salmon from the marinade and place on a well-oiled grill pan or grill. Broil 4 inches from heat for 4-6 minutes per ½-inch thickness. If the fish is more than an inch thick, turn it over half way through cooking. The salmon is done when it flakes easily. Remove salmon from the pan and chill in refrigerator until you are ready to assemble the salad.

for the salad

2 packages of organic field greens or
    spring mix
4 hard cooked eggs
½ pound blanched green beans
1 pint cherry tomatoes
½ pound mixed black and green olives
½ cup toasted pine nuts
½ cup Parmesan cheese
Freshly ground black pepper

Wash and dry the field greens. Boil the 4 eggs and when cooled, peel and cut them into wedges. Blanch the green beans in boiling water for 4 minutes and remove promptly to an ice water bath. When beans are cooled, pat them dry. Wash and dry the cherry tomatoes. Toast pine nuts in a dry sauté pan until lightly golden. Shred the Parmesan cheese.

vinaigrette

¾ cup olive oil
¼ cup balsamic vinegar
Salt and pepper to taste

Put olive oil and balsamic vinegar in a glass jar or bowl, add salt and pepper to taste and whisk together until completely emulsified.

assembling the salad

Add field greens to a large bowl and drizzle with the vinaigrette. Toss well, coating all of the greens. Spread the greens on a large platter. Add the pieces of cooked salmon over the greens. Arrange the egg wedges, green beans and tomatoes over the salad and scatter the olives and pine nuts over the top. Sprinkle with the Parmesan cheese. Drizzle more of the vinaigrette over the assembled salad and grind fresh black pepper over it all.

– serves 8

tortellini salad in pesto

Pesto comes from Italy's Liguria region—more specifically from the Cinque Terre, five fishing villages clinging to the rocky Ligurian coast. When visiting there on our culinary tours, we often smell the pesto in the restaurant before we can see it. Garlic, pine nuts, and two kinds of cheese are added to the sweet basil that grows profusely in the area, along with extra virgin olive oil to make a creamy sauce for our pasta.

I enjoy making pesto in the summer when you can buy basil inexpensively at the farmer's markets. Better yet, grow your own and make pesto from your own crop. Make several batches and freeze it, enabling you to enjoy a taste of summer all winter long. Thaw a frozen container of pesto in warm water and toss it over pasta or spread over a panino.

pesto sauce

2 cups fresh basil, washed and dried
4 medium-sized cloves of garlic, chopped
1 cup pine nuts, lightly toasted
1 cup freshly grated Parmesan cheese
¼ cup Romano cheese
Salt and pepper to taste
1 cup best quality extra virgin olive oil

Process the basil, garlic and pine nuts in the bowl of a food processor fitted with a steel blade. Add the cheeses, a big pinch of salt, and a liberal grinding of pepper. With the machine running, add the oil in a steady stream. Process briefly to combine. If sauce seems too thick, add a bit more oil. Remove to a storage bowl and cover with a light layer of olive oil until ready to use. (This preserves the pesto's bright green color.)

tortellini

1 pound fresh cheese- or chicken-filled tortellini

Cook tortellini according to package directions. Saving 1 cup of the cooking water, drain tortellini well. In a large serving bowl add the tortellini and a small amount of pesto at a time, gently tossing and adding pesto until the tortellini is well coated. If the sauce seems too thick, add a bit of the warm cooking liquid to smooth it out. When the pasta is well coated with pesto, grind black pepper over the top and pass a bowl of grated Parmesan cheese around. Additional toasted pine nuts and a sprig of basil can be added to each serving.

– serves 8

✦

CARMELA COMMENTS | Grilled or roasted chicken cut into strips can be added to the pasta to make this a main course salad.

lemon and polenta cake with fresh berries

This recipe is from my business partner, Doris Fortino. It's a wonderful summer dessert when served with fresh berries, but can also be enjoyed in the fall with a compote of apples and raisins or pears and dried cranberries. The subtle lemon flavor of the cake lends itself to many combinations. The olive oil keeps the cake moist, while the canola oil lightens the batter a bit. Doris makes it as a single layer cake. However, you could double the recipe and put the batter in two round cake pans to be served as a layer cake, with lemon curd in the center and whipped cream frosting. Our guests love this easy-to-make cake, and I hope your guests will too.

2 lemons
4 eggs
¾ cup granulated sugar
1¾ cup all purpose flour
3 teaspoons baking powder
Pinch of salt
¾ cup olive oil
¾ cup canola oil
⅔ cup polenta (cornmeal)
Confectioners' sugar
Summer berries or other fruit
½ pint whipping cream, whipped

Zest the lemons and set zest aside. Place lemons in a pan, add water to cover, and bring to a boil, simmering for about 10 minutes. Drain lemons and, when cool enough, squeeze pulp and juice into a bowl, removing any seeds.

In a large mixing bowl beat the eggs until light. Add granulated sugar and beat another 2-3 minutes. Sift together the flour, baking powder and salt. Slowly add this to the egg and sugar mixture while gently mixing. Add the olive and canola oils and blend well. When well mixed, add the polenta, lemon pulp, juice and zest and mix again.

Grease a 9-inch spring form pan and line the bottom with parchment paper. Pour the cake batter into the prepared pan and bake at 350 degrees for about 50 minutes, or until a toothpick inserted in the center comes out clean. When cake is cool remove it from the pan and place it on a beautiful platter. Dust with confectioners' sugar and serve with fresh berries and whipped cream.

– serves 12

Wine Pairings

The symphony of flavors and textures captured in this menu calls for a pairing with some character. Given the likely warm weather setting, this is another occasion for suggesting a nicely chilled dry rosé. With the salmon salad entre, a rosé of Pinot Noir (such as from Raptor Ridge) would be excellent. For those with a yen for something French, the Domaine Font de Michelle from the Cotes du Rhone is just the ticket. Librandi's "Ciro Rosato" is another fine option for this luncheon.

On the white wine side, a good Vermentino will marry beautifully with all of these dishes—especially the salmon salad and the tortellini in pesto. Sardinia accounts for some of the best of this varietal to be found here. Try the Sella & Mosca Vermentino di Sardegna "La Cala" or the Argiolas "Costamolino." While it may be a bit harder to find, the Poggio al Tufo Vermentino bottled by Tommasi, in Tuscany's Marrema region, would be well worth seeking out.

Dinner at Tursi's Latin King

ANTIPASTI OF ITALIAN MEATS, CHEESES
AND MARINATED VEGETABLES
ANGEL HAIR PASTA IN AMOGIO SAUCE
CHICKEN SPIEDINI
FRESH-ROASTED ASPARAGUS
LATIN KING CANNOLI

"*Una Tradizione Italiana*" is how Tursi's Latin King restaurant is described. Originally established by our cousins Rose and Jimmy Pigneri in 1947, my younger brother Bobby and his wife Amy have owned this Des Moines, Iowa, landmark since 1983, when he was only 21 years old. Now, with nearly 30 years of experience under his belt, Bobby claims that the secret to success is a strong work ethic. (I suspect the quality of the food has something to do with it, too.) Inspired by our father, Joe (an Italian immigrant from Terravecchia, Italy), Bobby, Amy, and their son R.J. continue to serve up true Italian hospitality.

The Latin King has served as the back-drop to many of our family celebrations. In 1950 my parents, their family and friends enjoyed their wedding luncheon at the restaurant—then owned by our cousins. My aunts hosted my own bridal shower there in 1974. The Latin King's famous fried chicken was on the menu that day, to everyone's delight. I was showered with beautiful gifts, love and support from a wonderful group of aunts, cousins and friends.

Today we host groom's dinners and baptismal lunches there, and our son Patrick and his friends were honored with a celebration after his graduation from medical school. Just about any special event in our growing family is held within the walls of the Latin King. The same could be said for many of the customers who line up early in the evening for a table there.

The Latin King continues to honor the Tursi family name and is regarded as the best Italian restaurant in central Iowa by local press and dining enthusiasts. It is with great pleasure that I present to you, Dinner at Tursi's Latin King.

antipasti of meats, cheeses, and marinated vegetables

*I*talians generally start their meals with a little antipasti to "open the stomach" to receive the meal that follows. You can use any combination of Italian meats, cheeses, olives and other marinated vegetables that you wish. You'll want to have a good supply of crusty, warm bread and crisp crostini available to enjoy with this antipasti.

    I suggest that you visit a good Italian market and select an assortment that appeals to you from the deli case. Just make sure that the meats and cheeses are sliced thin or that the cheese is cut into large wedges from which your guests can cut their own portions.

Leaf lettuce
1 (6 ounce) can of Italian tuna in olive oil
8 ounces of salami or other cured meats, thinly sliced
8 ounces of prosciutto, thinly sliced
8 ounces of provolone cheese, thinly sliced
8 ounces of small fresh mozzarella balls (*bococinni*)
1 cup marinated olives
1 cup marinated artichokes
1 cup marinated mushrooms

Layer several crisp lettuce leaves on a large platter. Drain the tuna and place it in the center of the platter. Lay the sliced meats and cheeses around the tuna. If you select wedges of cheese, add them to the platter as well. Carefully place the mozzarella balls, olives, artichokes and mushrooms in groups around the platter. Serve with bread, crostini or crackers.

– serves 8-12

angel hair pasta in amogio sauce

*T*his is simple, light pasta that is just tossed with the same Amogio sauce used for the chicken spiedini. It can be easily doubled to feed more people. Any long thin pasta will work with this sauce. Make sure to garnish it with a good handful of freshly

grated Parmesan cheese and chopped parsley. For an
added kick, add a bit of dried red pepper flakes.

1 pound angel hair pasta
Amogio sauce (see below)
Parmesan cheese
Chopped fresh parsley

Cook pasta in rapidly boiling salted water until
al dente. Be careful not to overcook the pasta. Toss
with some of the Amogio sauce, freshly grated Parmesan cheese and chopped fresh parsley.

– serves 4

amogio sauce

1 cup extra virgin olive oil
½ cup dry white wine
½ cup lemon juice
3 cloves garlic chopped
2 tablespoons kosher salt
Pinch of dried red pepper flakes
¼ cup finely chopped fresh basil

Mix all of the above ingredients together until emulsified. Let stand briefly for flavors to mingle. Drizzle over the chicken spiedini and toss the remaining
sauce (or a portion of it) with the angel hair pasta.

chicken spiedini

According to Pat Morris, chef at the Latin King, this recipe for chicken spiedini has been their single best seller for more than 15 years. Boneless breast of chicken is skewered and marinated, then coated in Italian breadcrumbs and charbroiled. It is served with Tursi's unique Amogio sauce.

8 single boneless chicken breasts cut into
    1-inch cubes
¾ cup dried breadcrumbs
¾ cup Parmesan cheese

marinade for the chicken

1 cup canola oil
½ cup dry white wine
¾ cup freshly squeezed lemon juice
10 cloves of garlic, finely minced
2 tablespoons kosher salt

Cut each chicken breast into 1-inch cubes and thread the cubes on skewers.

Mix together canola oil, dry white wine, lemon juice, garlic and salt. Place skewers in a non-reactive container and pour the marinade over them. Let them marinate in the fridge overnight.

When you're ready to cook, mix the breadcrumbs and Parmesan cheese together in a 9x13-inch glass pan. Shake off excess marinade from the chicken and then roll the skewers in the breadcrumb mixture. Let them rest for at least 30 minutes or up to an hour. The coating may become wet, which is fine. Cook over medium-high heat on a grill, turning often, until the chicken is completely cooked through and browned nicely. You may also bake them in an oven at 475 degrees for about 15 minutes, turning once. Allow breadcrumbs to brown. Drizzle the cooked chicken with Amogio sauce and serve.

– serves 8

fresh-roasted asparagus

Fresh asparagus can now be found at the market year around. Buy the freshest asparagus you can find, with tight tips. Roast only for a few minutes. You'll want it to have a bit of crunch left when you bite into the spears.

2 pounds fresh asparagus
¼ cup extra virgin olive oil
Salt
Freshly ground pepper

Cut or break off the tough ends of the asparagus spears. Lay the spears out on a baking sheet and drizzle with extra virgin olive oil. Then sprinkle with salt and pepper. Toss the spears until they are well coated. Roast in a 400 degree oven for about 10 minutes.

– serves 8

latin king cannoli

Cannoli have been on the menu at the Latin King for years. This recipe has been changed a few times and improved by my sister-in-law, Amy Tursi. She substitutes cream cheese for some of the usual ricotta, resulting in a smoother consistency. Many happy family celebrations, from my parents wedding luncheon to family bridal showers and many birthday parties, have been held at the restaurant. Cannoli are always on the menu for these celebratory meals.

2 (8 ounce) packages cream cheese at
    room temperature
½ cup ricotta cheese
2 tablespoons sour cream
6 tablespoons whipping cream
1 tablespoon granulated sugar
1 tablespoon freshly squeezed lemon juice
1 cup confectioners' sugar
1 ounce semi-sweet chocolate, chopped
1 teaspoon vanilla extract
1 box of cannoli shells
Grated lemon zest for garnish
½ cup chopped pistachios

In a large mixing bowl blend together the cheeses, sour cream, whipping cream and the granulated sugar until smooth. Zest a lemon and reserve. Add lemon juice, confectioners' sugar, chopped chocolate and vanilla extract, and blend well.

Transfer mixture to a pastry bag and stuff the cannoli shells. Garnish with lemon zest or chopped pistachios. Refrigerate until ready to serve.

– serves 12

Wine Pairings

While the chicken spiedini traditionally calls for a white wine, the richness of the Amogio sauce requires something with substantial body of its own. This is, once again, a great place for a Chardonnay, such as Cambria's "Katherine's Vineyard," Sonoma-Cutrer "Sonoma Coast" or La Crema.

For the more adventurous, a lovely Viognier will pair beautifully with this menu. Made from a temperamental grape originating in the Rhone Valley near Lyon, this wine has only recently been mastered in this country. Its intensely floral aromas and balanced acidity make for a great drinking experience, especially with richer foods. Among the best domestic offerings of this wine are Cold Heaven "Le Bon Climat" from Santa Barbara and Witness Tree from Oregon.

At the Latin King itself, the preferred pairing for this menu is Librandi's "Critone," a delightful blend of Chardonnay and Sauvignon Blanc grapes.

PROSCIUTTO AND MELON WRAPS

BLUE CHEESE AND HONEY BRUSCHETTA

ORANGE AND BLUEBERRY SALAD

ORANGE-BRINED SMOKED TURKEY

SURPRISE MASHED POTATOES

ROASTED ROOT VEGETABLES WITH BALSAMIC GLAZE

CRANBERRY RELISH

ALMOND PEAR TART

CRANBERRY CAKE

Thanksgiving is my favorite holiday; it's all about the food. No presents to open or tree to decorate. While this menu is basically set, I do like to try out a few new things each year. Growing up in an Italian-American family, the turkey was always secondary to the pasta dishes that my mother prepared. For this Thanksgiving meal, the turkey reigns supreme. When he was young, our son Teddy always gave the turkey a name; soon we'll be passing that tradition on to our grandchildren.

It's easy to over-indulge on Thanksgiving, so I've thrown in a few light recipes that are favorites at our house. Try my take on melon proscuitto, surprise mashed potatoes or poached fruit.

I love to have a crowd for this special day, which means I have to be well-organized. Weeks ahead, I set the menu and purchase pantry items. I get the silver polished, press the napkins and tablecloth, and get the good china, crystal and silver out and ready for the big day. Early in the week I make another run to the market to pick up the remaining fresh items.

I don't try to do all the work myself but assign portions of the meal to others to prepare, or let my guests help me during the day. We all love to cook and enjoy being in the kitchen together. With careful organization and planning I find that I'm not stressed but well rested. This allows me to enjoy this festive holiday, full of gratitude for the many blessings I've enjoyed during the year.

prosciutto and melon wraps

This is a classic Italian antipasto with a new twist. I like serving something light and simple such as the prosciutto and melon wraps before a big heavy meal. It is just meant to "open the stomach," as my grandfather would say, to receive the larger meal, which Thanksgiving dinner always seems to be. Use the very best quality olive oil and well-aged balsamic vinegar to drizzle over the dish.

1½ cantaloupes, cut in half, seeds removed
¾ pound prosciutto, thinly sliced
Extra virgin olive oil
Aged balsamic vinegar
Freshly ground black pepper

Cut each cantaloupe in half and remove the seeds. Cut each half of melon into thin slices and peel. Cut each of the slices of prosciutto in half lengthwise. Wrap a piece of prosciutto around the cantaloupe. Drizzle with the extra virgin olive oil and balsamic vinegar and grind fresh black pepper over the plate.

– serves 12

✦

CARMELA COMMENTS | Honey Dew melon could be used instead of cantaloupe.

blue cheese and honey bruschetta

*M**ake the crostini for this recipe earlier in the week. Just before your guests arrive, top them with the blue cheese and honey. This recipe is so simple, yet so delicious.*

> 1 baguette cut into 24 pieces
> olive oil
> 4 ounces of blue cheese
> 3 tablespoons best quality honey, such as
>   lavender infused

Cut the baguette into 24 pieces. Brush both sides of each slice with olive oil and place on a baking sheet. Broil the bread for 1 to 2 minutes on each side or until golden. Cool and set aside until serving time. Bring the blue cheese to room temperature and then spread the cheese over the crostini and drizzle with the honey.

– serves 12

Wine Pairings

The smoked turkey, with its notes of citrus from the brining process, is the focal point of the wine pairings for this celebration. Pinot Noir, having its own smoky undertones, provides the perfect choice for a red wine. Oregon's Willamette Valley turns out some of the most consistently superb Pinot Noir in this country. Having gone to the trouble of brining and smoking your bird to perfection, this may be a time to splurge a bit for an especially nice wine. While you can certainly spend a great deal more, let me suggest Four Graces "Reserve" Pinot Noir, Witness Tree "Vintage Select," or Argyle's "Willamette." Very good and slightly more affordable options from California include "A" by Acacia Vineyards and DeLoach Vineyards' "Russian River."

For a white wine pairing, we always select a slightly sweet Gewürztraminer, one of the signature wines of Alsace. It complements the apple-wood smoked turkey beautifully. Among our favorites are Trimbach and Pierre Sparr. For a domestic option, try the offering from Banyan in Monterey County, California.

Given the special place of Thanksgiving among our family's traditions, we always offer both of these varietals for our guests.

orange and blueberry salad

Susan Lukens was the food stylist for my first cookbook, Carmela's Cucina, and she also introduced me to my publisher, Norton Stillman. At the time of our meeting she had just released her own fondue cookbook with Nodin Press. Over the years, Susan became a friend and advised me so much about writing cookbooks and creating recipes.

Susan passed away recently following a long illness. This recipe comes from her book, Let's Fondue. We all miss Susan, but she lives on through the work she created as a cook, an author, and a talented food stylist. I will always be grateful to her for the role she played in getting my work published.

This light, colorful salad is perfect for a large Thanksgiving dinner, though I use it all year long and everyone loves it. For a short cut, I sometimes use Mandarin oranges.

1 pint fresh blueberries
¼ cup packed light brown sugar
2 tablespoons balsamic vinegar
2 tablespoons finely minced red onion
Pinch of salt
8 cups Spring Mix lettuces
5 navel oranges, peeled and sliced
4 tablespoons extra virgin olive oil
Coarsely ground black pepper to taste
½ cup toasted pecans or walnuts, chopped

Rinse and drain the blueberries. In a large bowl, whisk together the sugar, vinegar, onion, and salt. Gently mix in the blueberries. Cover and refrigerate for 30 minutes or up to 2 days.

Spread the Spring Mix evenly over a large platter. Peel the oranges, removing as much of the white membrane and possible. Cut the oranges into thin slices. Place the oranges in a wide circle on the bed of greens, slightly overlapping.

With a slotted spoon, scoop the blueberries inside the circle of orange slices. Spoon the blueberry marinade over the salad and drizzle with the olive oil. Season with freshly ground black pepper. Scatter the chopped nuts over the oranges.

– makes 8 servings

surprise mashed potatoes

The surprise in this dish is that these are not potatoes at all, but heart-healthy cauliflower. I am always looking for ways to "lighten up" this calorie-laden meal. When my husband, Bob, suggested making this dish for Thanksgiving one year, I did. Guess what? No one missed the traditional mashed potatoes and gravy. I don't even make gravy anymore because the Surprise Mashed Potatoes are so tasty and the brined and smoked turkey so moist, you don't need it. The additional calories saved by skipping the gravy allows me to serve two desserts, both of which I have included on this menu.

This is one of the recipes that I use in my, "Italian Women Stay Slim" classes and everyone really does love it. You may never feel the need to make real mashed potatoes again.

8 cups of cauliflower florets
2 ounces of butter
2 ounces fat-free half-and-half
Salt and pepper to taste
Chopped flat leaf parsley for garnish

In a small amount of water steam the cauliflower until it's soft. In a food processor or blender, puree cauliflower, butter and half-and-half until smooth. Add salt and pepper to taste, garnish with parsley and serve.

– makes 8 servings

cranberry relish

Make this relish early in the week to let the flavors blend. I love it with our smoked turkey, but it is great with pork or chicken as well.

3 cups cranberries
1 cup sugar
1 tablespoon freshly chopped ginger
1 (15 ounce) can of Mandarin oranges, drained

Combine the cranberries, sugar and ginger in a large sauté pan and cook over medium heat, stirring occasionally, until sugar is melted and cranberries begin to pop, about 5 minutes.

Add 1 cup of water and simmer until liquid has thickened—about 4 minutes. Remove from heat and cool. Stir in drained Mandarin oranges.

– makes 3 cups

orange-brined smoked turkey

Years ago, after a fall trip to the Napa Valley, my husband Bob got it into his head that he was going to brine and smoke a turkey for Thanksgiving. Today this practice is highly recommended to keep your turkey moist, but at the time it was all but unheard of. I was initially very resistant to the idea. We were having a large group of people for dinner that year, and I didn't want to be trying something new. Our compromise was to have a "turkey cook-off." We'd both prepare one and then decide which was better.

I was boasting to anyone who would listen about the likely outcome of this cook-off, confident of the superiority of my time-honored methods. Bob was remarkably quiet about his plan. He purchased the required ingredients on his own and started brining the turky on the Sunday before Thanksgiving. On Thanksgiving Day he was up at 5:00 a.m. preparing the smoker, and the bird was cooking inside it long before I was out of bed.

I prepared my turkey as always, taking care to massage the butter and herbs into its skin, placing it in a large roasting pan and giving it a blessing. When we finally served up our turkeys, hours later, it was easy to see that everyone preferred Bob's, which was browned beautifully, moist throughout, and quite flavorful—unlike my pale, dried-up bird.

Now, years later, Bob remains in charge of the main course for this meal, rising early to get the bird in the smoker, while I sleep peacefully. When I rise to start getting side dishes ready, I'm greeted by the most amazing smell of the turkey smoking away, right outside my kitchen window.

This recipe has a long list of ingredients. Don't let this keep you from trying this recipe because the end result is a really moist, tender turkey with a subtle blend of spicy and citrusy flavors. We use a cylindrical, electric smoker. Bob feels that apple wood chunks work best, but we have also used hickory. If you don't have a smoker, brine your bird using my directions and roast it as you usually would or use a kettle-type grill to cook it.

1 gallon of orange juice
2 cups of rice wine vinegar
2 cups of apple cider vinegar
1 cup dark brown sugar
6 cloves of garlic crushed
¼ cup sliced fresh ginger
1 bunch green onions, sliced
2 bunches cilantro, chopped
12 whole star anise
2 cinnamon sticks, crushed
2 tablespoons red pepper flakes
1 tablespoon whole cloves
2 tablespoons whole black peppercorns
1 cup kosher salt
1 (12-15 pound) turkey with the giblets
   and neck removed
2 pounds apple wood chips for smoking
   (or hickory chips)
Extra virgin olive oil
Salt and pepper to taste

Combine the orange juice, rice wine vinegar, apple cider vinegar, brown sugar, garlic, ginger, green onion, cilantro, star anise, cinnamon, red pepper flakes, cloves, peppercorns and salt in a stock pot. Bring to a boil, reduce heat to low and simmer for 45 minutes. Let cool. The brine can be prepared ahead and refrigerated in a nonmetal container.

Thoroughly rinse and dry the turkey inside and out. Place the turkey in a large plastic, glass or earthenware container that is not much wider than the turkey and deep enough so that the brine will cover it. Do not use a metal container. Pour the brine over the turkey and refrigerate it for 3 days. If the brine does not completely cover the turkey, you will have to turn it every 12 hours.

Soak the wood chips for the smoking in water for at least 30 minutes, well before starting the smoker or grill. This can be done the night before cooking.

Remove the turkey from the brining liquid and dry it inside and out. Place it on a on a roasting rack and rub with extra virgin olive oil, salt and pepper.

If you're using a kettle grill rather than a smoker, place a drip pan on the fire grate of grill. Place 20 or 30 briquettes on either side of the pan. Light and let the briquettes burn until coated with white ash—about 30 minutes.

Place the turkey in the center of the grill cooking rack over the drip pan. Place small handfuls of wet wood chips on the hot briquettes. Cover kettle with the lid. Partially open lid and kettle vents. Try not to open the lid too often, which will lower the temperature, but check the turkey about every 45 minutes. Replenish briquettes as needed, adding about 10 each time, along with additional wood chips.

If the turkey gets too dark, cover with foil. Smoke the turkey on the kettle grill for 2½ to 3 hours or until a meat thermometer inserted in the thickest part of the breast and not touching the bone reaches

165-170 degrees. When using a smoker, follow the directions with your unit, as this will take much longer on most kettle grills. If cooking the turkey in the oven, follow the directions that come with it. Carefully transfer the turkey to a carving platter and let it rest for about 20 minutes before carving.

– serves 12-15

✦

CARMELA COMMENTS | Bob likes to use a fresh turkey for this recipe. He also will cut oranges, onions, apples or lemons into quarters and insert them into the cavity of the turkey for additional flavor and to keep the turkey even more moist. Remember you must begin brining your turkey early in the week.

roasted root vegetables with balsamic vinegar

I love the earthy flavor of these vegetables. The vegetables can be washed, peeled and cut the day before and roasted the day you are serving them. Try to cut everything the same size so that they cook evenly. I like to use different colored beets for a nice variety. If there are any vegetables left over, they're excellent served cold.

2 large parsnips, peeled and cut into
    1-inch chunks
2 turnips, peeled and cut into 1-inch chunks
1 rutabaga, peeled and cut into 1-inch chunks
4 large carrots, peeled and cut into
    1-inch chunks
1 pound small beets, peeled and quartered
¼ cup extra virgin olive oil
¼ cup balsamic vinegar
Salt and pepper to taste

Preheat the oven to 400 degrees. Put the cut parsnips, turnips, rutabaga, carrots and beets in a roasting pan large enough to hold all of the vegetables in a single layer. Pour the olive oil over the vegetables and toss to coat evenly. Bake for 45 minutes, or until the vegetables are almost tender and juices are caramelized. Pour the balsamic vinegar over the vegetables and sprinkle with a generous amount of salt and pepper. Toss to coat evenly. Return to the oven and bake for an additional 10 to 15 minutes, stirring once or twice to distribute the juices evenly during cooking.

– serves 8

almond pear tart

This tart is a combination of several recipes I have used over the years in my cooking classes. What I like about the crust is that you pat it into the tart pan, rather than having to roll it out. The almond pastry cream puffs up and turns a beautiful golden brown color as it bakes around the fruit. The poached pears in the tart are wonderful on their own. Double the recipe and just have some poached fruit for those people who might be actually calorie counting during this meal. Other fruits such as apples or peaches could also be used for this delicious tart.

for the crust

1½ sticks butter
⅓ cup sugar
½ teaspoon pure almond extract
1½ cups all-purpose flour

In an electric mixer, beat butter and sugar together for 4 or 5 minutes, or until pale and fluffy. Reduce speed to low and add almond extract, followed by flour. Mix until crumbly.

Transfer the dough to a 10x1-inch round tart pan that has been sprayed with cooking spray, such as Pam. Spread dough over the bottom of the pan. Place a large piece of plastic wrap over the dough and press it evenly on the bottom and up the sides of the pan.

for the almond cream

½ cup (1 stick) butter
½ cup sugar
¾ cup blanched, finely ground almonds
¼ cup dark rum (reserve 1 tablespoon)
1 large egg
1 teaspoon pure almond extract
1 tablespoon all-purpose flour

Combine butter and sugar in the bowl of an electric mixer fitted with a paddle attachment. Beat until light and fluffy, about 2 minutes. In a food processor grind the almonds. Add ground almonds, 3 tablespoons rum, egg, almond extract, and flour to the butter and sugar, and beat until smooth. Spread the almond cream evenly into the tart shell.

for the white-wine poached pears

2 cups white wine, Champagne, or
    sparkling white wine
1 cup sugar
Juice and zest of 1 lemon
1 cinnamon stick
1 vanilla bean, split
4 firm but ripe Bartlett pears, peeled,
    with stem left on

Combine wine with 4 cups of water, sugar, lemon juice, lemon zest, cinnamon stick and vanilla bean in a large pot. Bring contents to a boil, and cook for 5 minutes. Add pears, reduce to a simmer, and cook until the pears are tender when pierced with a knife—about 20-30 minutes. Cool pears in poaching liquid.

assembling

Remove cooled, poached pears from liquid, and cut each in half lengthwise, removing core and stem. Place each half, cut side down, on a cutting board, and cut crosswise into thin slices. Arrange sliced pear halves on almond pastry cream around the edge of tart, leaving space between each half, and place one half in the center of the tart. When arranging pears, try to stretch slices toward center of tart, which will elongate pears a bit and fill the shell better. Bake in a 375 degree oven for 40 to 45 minutes or until the almond cream is puffed and brown.

for the glaze

Reserved 1 tablespoon rum
½ cup apricot jam

While the tart is baking, melt apricot jam with remaining tablespoon rum in a small saucepan over medium heat. While still warm, brush the pear tart with apricot rum glaze. Cool tart to room temperature before slicing.

– serves 12

♦

CARMELA COMMENTS | You could double this recipe and serve the pears well chilled for those people who are calorie-counting, or for dessert on another occasion. And for those who do not want to use alcohol, you could use sparkling grape juice.

cranberry cake

This cake is so easy that with some adult supervision your children could make it. It freezes well, and we enjoy it all year long as a coffee cake. Just make sure that you always have some frozen cranberries in your freezer. Mixing the cranberries and walnuts with the sugar and some flour keeps them from sinking to the bottom of the cake. Cranberries and walnuts were, in my opinion, created to go together, and this rich coffee cake proves my point.

2 cups chopped cranberries
½ cup chopped walnuts
½ cup sugar
1 cup flour
2 large eggs
¾ cup melted butter, cooled
1 cup sugar
¼ teaspoon salt
¼ teaspoon pure almond extract
Confectioners' sugar for dusting

Mix the cranberries and nuts with ½ cup sugar and a small amount of flour. Beat together the eggs, cooled melted butter, 1 cup sugar until smooth. Add flour, salt and pure almond extract. Fold the cranberry mixture into the cake batter and combine.

Pour the batter into a well greased 10-inch spring form pan. Bake in a preheated 350 degree oven for 40 minutes in the center of the oven. Test with a toothpick to make sure the batter is cooked through. When cake is cooled, dust with confectioners' sugar.

– serves 12

Clockwise from upper left: orzo salad (p. 68), mini-frittatas (p. 54), crab salad martini (p. 62), marinated summer tomatoes (p. 65), and buttered carrots (p. 144).

SEAFOOD ANTIPASTO

SARDINE SPREAD

TUNA CREAM IN PHYLLO CUPS

LINGUINE WITH CLAM SAUCE

FILLET OF COD FLORENTINE

CAULIFLOWER SALAD

SLICED ORANGES ON A BED OF ARUGULA

TUSCAN BREAD PUDDING WITH AMARETTO SAUCE

During my childhood and adolescence, the family Christmas Eve celebration invariably included a meal with the traditional Seven Fish. As a child I didn't like this tradition at all. "Who would serve seven different fish for a holiday?" I always asked. In those days Christmas Eve was a day of fasting and abstinence—no meat. While my non-Catholic friends were dining on turkey, ham, and rib roasts, I was doomed to eating seven fish.

As I grew older I began to question my grandmothers and my mother about the tradition. Why seven? Which fish need to be included? What does the tradition have to do with the birth of Jesus? But no one could give me the answers. They simply replied that their mothers before them made the seven fish and the tradition must carry on, and so it did.

As a young adult I began to take on more of the holiday preparations myself, and I became still more inquisitive about this holiday tradition. I learned from an expert at the Italian consulate in Philadelphia that this tradition is still well kept in southern Italy. I understand that thirteen dishes are commonly served, seven of which should be fish. The fish used are baccala (salt codfish), calamari, eel, mussels, clams, sardines, and octopus.

Today, in my home, we may or may not have all seven fish, but we always have some—usually a shrimp cocktail that we all devour before my mother has even finished cooking the baccala and the stuffed calamari (for those recipes see pages 93 and 96 of *Carmela's Cucina*, my first cookbook). Since the Church has relaxed its rules to permit meat to be eaten on Christmas Eve, we now serve dishes with meat as well.

Why seven fish? I still don't have the answer. Some say for the seven days of the week, others say it recalls the seven sacraments of the Catholic Church or even the seven gifts of the Holy Spirit. Whatever the symbolism, I've grown to like the idea because it is tradition. So I always serve some fish on Christmas Eve. In some small way it makes me feel as though I'm connecting my family to their Italian roots.

seafood antipasto

This antipasto is not only a wonderful primi course, but it can stand alone as a light lunch or dinner. With a loaf of crusty bread, it makes a nice meal. Do not let the long list of ingredients keep you from trying this recipe. It all goes together very quickly. It is best if prepared a day ahead so that the seafood has a chance to marinate with the other ingredients.

7 tablespoons olive oil, divided
12 ounces sea scallops
12 ounces medium shrimp, shelled and deveined
2 teaspoons fresh lemon juice
1 pound cod fillets, cut into cubes
1 tablespoon sugar
1 tablespoon minced dry onion
1 teaspoon salt
½ teaspoon garlic powder
½ teaspoon freshly ground black pepper
½ teaspoon red pepper flakes
1 cup fresh basil leaves, divided
1 (6 ounce) can small pitted black olives, drained
1 (6 ounce) jar stuffed Spanish green olives, drained
1 (5 ounce) jar artichoke hearts, drained
8 ounces mushroom caps, cleaned and quartered
12 ounces of mozzarella, cut into 1-inch cubes
4 ounces cherry tomatoes, cut in half
1 cup good quality extra virgin olive oil
⅔ cup balsamic vinegar
Crisp salad greens
Basil leaves for garnish

over the basil. Add the seafood and top with olives, mushrooms, artichokes, and cheese. Top with the remaining sugar mixture and ½ cup of basil leaves.

Combine olive oil and vinegar and pour over basil and seafood mixture. Cover and refrigerate overnight. To serve, discard the top layer of basil leaves. Using a slotted spoon, remove the seafood mixture from the pan and place on a platter lined with salad greens. Garnish with fresh basil leaves.

—serves 12

♦

Heat 4 tablespoons of olive oil in a large non-stick skillet over high heat. Add scallops, cook and stir for 2 to 4 minutes until scallops are opaque. Remove from heat and put into a bowl. Add shrimp to the pan and cook about 5 minutes or until the shrimp turn opaque and are firm to the touch. Combine the shrimp and scallops, and stir in the lemon juice. Set aside.

Heat remaining 3 tablespoons of olive oil over high heat in another large non-stick skillet. Add cod, and cook, stirring 1 to 2 minutes until cod is opaque. Remove from the skillet and set aside.

Combine sugar, onion, salt, garlic powder, black pepper and red pepper flakes in a small bowl. Place ½ cup of basil leaves in the bottom of a 13x9 inch Pyrex pan and sprinkle half of the sugar mixture

CARMELA COMMENTS | When cleaning mushroom caps, use a damp paper towel or a mushroom brush. Never put mushrooms in water or clean them under running water.

sardine spread

Make this easy spread early in the day so that all of the flavors have a chance to mingle and blend. The spread can be put on top of crostini or piped into celery.

2 tins of boned, skinless sardines in oil
4 tablespoons unsalted butter
1 tablespoon lemon juice
2 tablespoons Dijon mustard
1 tablespoon chopped parsley
Salt and pepper to taste
Celery stalks, cut into pieces
1 tablespoon capers, drained

Put contents of sardine tins in blender. Add butter, lemon juice, mustard, and parsley and blend until creamy. Add salt and pepper if needed.

Spread mixture on celery pieces and top with capers. Refrigerate until ready to serve.

– serves 8

tuna cream in phyllo cups

The recipe for this wonderful and easy anti-pasto was given to me by the cook at Villa La Volpe in Tuscany, where my culinary tour groups stay for a week while we tour the area. As the group is out hiking in the Cinque Terre, Doctor Daniela Grossi's top-notch cook, Maria, is whipping up a multi-course dinner for us to enjoy when we return. As we dine outdoors on a warm fall evening, Tuna in Phyllo Cups is usually the first antipasto served to us while we sip a glass of wine and enjoy the Tuscan moon.

2 (6 ounce) cans of Italian-style tuna
½ cup butter (1 stick), softened
⅓ cup mayonnaise
2 tablespoons of capers
2 packages Athens mini-phyllo shells (15 count)
1 small jar of pimento stuffed olives, drained

Drain tuna and add it to a food processor to blend with the softened butter. Add mayonnaise and pulse several times until the mixture is nice and smooth. Rinse and drain 2 tablespoons of capers. Add these to the mixture and pulse again until well blended.

Remove the tuna cream from the bowl of the processor, and fill a pastry bag fitted with a large tip with the tuna cream mixture. Pipe the cream into the phyllo shells just before serving. Garnish the tops of each tuna cream with an olive.

– makes 30

linguine with clam sauce

This is a classic dish from Italy. On my culinary tours, our guests enjoy this as a pasta course when we visit my favorite restaurant in the Cinque Terre, Bel Forte. Bel Forte uses fresh clams in their shells, brought in daily from the crystal waters of the Ligurian Sea.

The recipe that I offer you here is one that I've been making for years. It's taken from a cookbook assembled back in the 1970's by the parishioners of St. Anthony Church in Des Moines, Iowa, where I grew up. Contributed by Mrs. Michael (Anna) Graziano, this delicious pasta is as good today as the first time I tried it. The recipe calls for using canned minced clams, which I love, because it allows me to make this dish on the spur of the moment—I always have a few cans of clams and some dry pasta stored in my pantry.

1 (8 ounce) can minced clams
¼ cup extra virgin olive oil
2 cloves garlic, minced
1 (8 ounce) bottle clam juice
Black pepper
Pinch of dried oregano
Pinch of red pepper flakes
4 tablespoons butter
Handful of chopped parsley
1 pound cooked linguine

Drain the minced clams and reserve the liquid. In a sauté pan, add the olive oil and when hot add the garlic and cook until golden brown, being careful not to burn. Add the drained minced clams and heat through. Add the reserved liquid, clam juice, pepper, oregano, and red pepper flakes and simmer gently, uncovered, for 2 to 3 minutes. Remove the pan from the heat and stir in the butter. Pour the sauce over hot linguine, add the chopped parsley and toss well.

– serves 8 for pasta course or 4 for dinner course

✦

CARMELA COMMENTS | If using fresh clams, you will need about 3 or 4 pounds.

fillet of cod florentine

This dish, also from the St. Anthony cookbook, makes a perfect main course for a Christmas Eve dinner, but it would also be wonderful during Lent or at any time of the year. I use frozen chopped spinach for this recipe, avoiding the laborious preparation of using fresh. However, if you prefer, fresh spinach can be used instead.

8 small fillets of fresh cod
1½ cups dry white wine
1 stick butter, divided
2 (10 ounce) packages of frozen chopped
    spinach, defrosted
⅓ cup grated Parmesan cheese
1 cup Mornay Sauce

In a non-stick sauté pan, melt ½ stick butter. Add the cod fillets evenly in the pan and sprinkle with salt and pepper. Add the wine. Simmer for about 8 to 10 minutes. Remove fillets from the stove.

Squeeze the spinach dry. Melt the remaining butter in a sauté pan and add the spinach. Sauté until heated through.

In a 9x13-inch baking dish, spread out the spinach and lay the fillets on top. Cover the fillets with the Mornay Sauce and sprinkle with the Parmesan cheese. Place in a pre-heated 350 degree oven for about 15 to 20 minutes.

– serves 8

mornay sauce

4 tablespoons butter
1 tablespoon flour
1½ cups milk
½ teaspoon salt
2 tablespoons grated Parmesan cheese
1 egg yolk
Dash of white pepper
Dash of nutmeg

Melt butter in a small saucepan and add flour, stirring until it becomes a smooth paste; then slowly add milk. Stir continually while cooking over a low flame for 5 minutes. Sauce should have the consistency of thick cream. Add salt, pepper and nutmeg. Stir. Remove the sauce from the stove and stir in the cheese. Whip the egg yolk and quickly add to the sauce, stirring constantly. Pour the sauce over the fish and spinach.

– makes 1½ cups

cauliflower salad

This salad goes well with fish but is wonderful with any meal. I sometimes substitute broccoli for the cauliflower. If you want your salad extra spicy, add a pinch of red pepper flakes as my cousins in Calabria would do.

3 tablespoons chopped scallions
2 cloves garlic, chopped
1 teaspoon dried mustard
4 anchovy fillets, drained and chopped
¼ cup fresh lemon juice
1 tablespoon balsamic vinegar
¼ cup extra virgin olive oil
2 tablespoons capers, drained
1 head cauliflower, washed, trimmed
    and cut into florets
Salt and freshly ground black pepper to taste

Combine the scallions, garlic, mustard, anchovies, lemon juice, vinegar, and olive oil in the container of a blender or food processor. Process until well combined. Stir in the capers.

In a small amount of water over moderate heat, steam the cauliflower until tender but still crisp—about 7 minutes. Season it with salt and pepper, and transfer it to a serving dish. Pour the dressing over the cauliflower while it's still warm. Let stand for an hour and serve at room temperature.

– serves 8

sliced oranges on a bed of arugula

The oranges are a cool and sweet addition to this menu, providing a nice contrast to the fish. I suggest that you serve the oranges on a bed of arugula, but field greens would work equally well.

8 oranges
Zest of 1 lemon
½ cup fine granulated sugar
Juice of 2 oranges
Juice of 1 lemon
Arugula or field greens

Peel 6 of the oranges, removing the white membranes. Slice the oranges and put them into a shallow serving dish.

With a micro plane zest the lemon, then squeeze the juice of the lemon and the remaining oranges into a bowl. Add the sugar and mix well. Pour juice over the sliced oranges and coat them well.

Cover and refrigerate the oranges. At serving time, line a platter with arugula or field greens and arrange the orange slices over the top. Pour remaining juice over the oranges. Serve well chilled.

– serves 8

tuscan bread pudding
with amaretto sauce

This has to be my all-time favorite winter dessert. During the holiday season and over the winter months, my clients and guests frequently request this recipe. It's easy to make, and the Amaretto sauce could also be used over ice cream or pound cake. This recipe calls for panettone, which is a Christmas bread found all over Italy. Luckily, it's also easy to find here in the states during the holiday season. I always buy extra loaves and store them in my freezer so I can make this bread pudding whenever I want it. If you can't find panettone, any brioche-style bread would work. Just add some golden raisins and other dried fruit to the mixture. An unfrosted Norwegian Julekake would also be a good substitute.

1 *panettone* or other fruit-studded sweet
    bread (about 1 pound)
1 quart half-and-half
3 eggs
1 cup sugar
1 tablespoon plus 2 teaspoons vanilla extract
1 teaspoon almond extract
Amaretto sauce

Cut the *panettone* into 1-inch cubes and spread out on a cookie sheet to dry out for several hours or over night. When ready to make the bread pudding, add the dried bread cubes to a large mixing bowl and pour the half and half over the *panettone*. Make sure that all of the pieces are moistened. Set aside for about 1 hour until all the liquid has been absorbed.

Preheat the oven to 350 degrees. Generously butter the bottom and sides of a 9x13x2-inch baking dish or spray with cooking spray and set aside. In another mixing bowl, whisk the eggs with the sugar, vanilla, and almond extracts until well blended. Pour the egg mixture over the bread mixture and blend by hand. Transfer the mixture to the prepared baking dish and bake in the middle of the oven for about 1 hour, or until the pudding is set and the top is golden brown and puffy.

Preheat the broiler to the oven. Just before serving, spoon the Amaretto Sauce over the pudding and broil 3 to 4 inches from the heat until the sauce is bubbly and lightly browned. Cut the pudding into pieces.

– *serves 12*

✦

CARMELA COMMENTS | Use pure almond and vanilla extracts. The imitations tend to taste bitter. When broiling the pudding, watch closely as the sauce can burn easily.

amaretto sauce

1 stick unsalted butter, cut into pieces
1 cup confectioners' sugar
2 tablespoons Amaretto
2 egg yolks

In a double boiler, melt the butter. Slowly whisk in the confectioners' sugar until the mixture is creamy—about 30 seconds. Add the Amaretto and then the egg yolks, one at a time, whisking constantly. Cook the mixture until the sauce reaches 160 degrees—about 4 minutes—continuing to whisk. Let cool to room temperature. Pour the sauce over the bread pudding and broil until the sauce is caramelized, hot and bubbly.

✦

CARMELA COMMENTS | If you don't have a double boiler, use a medium bowl placed over a small saucepan. The pudding and sauce could be made one day ahead and refrigerated. At serving time, pour the sauce over the pudding and broil.

Wine Pairings

The wealth of fish and seafood anchoring this meal sends us to the Iberian peninsula for white wine pairings. The Albariño vines of the Rías Baixas DO of northwest Spain produce an intensely aromatic wine (think apricot and peach) with the high acidity needed to pair well with this varied seafood menu. (The same grape also grows in northwest Portugal, where it's called Alvarinho.) These wines have only recently begun to enjoy the following they deserve in this country, so you may need to visit a well-stocked shop. Our favorite Albariños to date have been Burgans and Martin Codax, both produced in Spain's Rías Baixas, and we're still enjoying the search!

The white wines of the Bucelas DOC in Portugal provide another excellent pairing for seafood dishes, especially those involving shellfish such as clams or mussels. These wines are the product of a blend of Arinto and Esgana Cao grapes grown in the region of Lisboa. Like Albariño, these wines are high in acidity and have modest alcohol content. The best labels I have found are Quinta da Murta, Quinta de Avelanda and Prova Regia.

These Iberian whites, which bring out the very best in fish and seafood, are likely to be among your "new favorites."

Christmas Day

JESSIE'S GOAT CHEESE STUFFED PEPPADEWS

GRAZZIETTA'S CHICKEN LIVER PATÉ

MARINATED BEEF TENDERLOIN

MADEIRA SAUCE

BRAISED BROCCOLI IN TOMATO CUPS

ENZA'S RISOTTO TRE COLORE

SICILIAN CASSATA

December is always such a busy month, with parties to give and open houses to attend. There is extra baking and food preparation to be completed; trees must be decorated and Christmas cards addressed, gifts purchased and wrapped, and special visits to loved ones are expected. I often wish that I could dedicate all my time in December to just "doing" Christmas, but there all also plenty of day-to-day tasks that won't go away. It's enough to put a girl in a bad mood. But I don't let the extra activities get the best of me. I'm well-organized, and I also know when to call in extra hands to help, while bringing some fun to the occasion as well.

This menu is wonderful because so many of the dishes can be prepared ahead by several days and then just put together on Christmas day after the gifts are open. The stuffed peppadews, which is a recipe that my daughter-in-law, Jessica, gave me, take just minutes to prepare, and the chicken liver paté can be made early in the week and stored in a fancy serving bowl. The beef tenderloin is best if marinated a day in advance, and both the broccoli in tomato cups and risotto can also be made in advance. Just remember to take everything out of the refrigerator for an hour or so to take the chill off before cooking, and you may have to adjust the cooking times a bit. Best of all, the cassata can be made several days in advance, allowing all the flavors to blend.

Relax and enjoy this special day with your family and friends. Give everyone a task—you'll feel less stressed and they'll be happy to help you. We have the children stick candles into the cassata, sing a few Christmas carols (including "Happy Birthday" to the infant Jesus), and put His figurine into the Christmas crèche. Most of all, remember the reason for this joyous season.

jessie's goat-cheese-stuffed peppadews

My daughter-in-law Jessica brought this anti-pasto to a family celebration one year, and we all loved it. The bright red color of this fruit from South Africa and the garnish of green chives make a very festive beginning to your Christmas dinner. Prepare them early in the day and place the stuffed peppadews on a lettuce-lined silver platter at serving time.

24 peppadews, drained and dried
6 ounces herbed goat cheese
Best quality honey to taste
2 tablespoons fresh chives, chopped
Leaf lettuce to garnish platter

Drain and dry peppadews. In a bowl mix the herbed goat cheese with the honey to taste. Place the mixture in a pastry bag or plastic bag. Fill the peppadews with the goat cheese mixture. Place the stuffed peppadews on a lettuce lined serving platter and garnish with the chopped chives.

serves 8

✦

CARMELA COMMENTS | You will find peppadews in the deli area of your store or near the olives. Save the juice from the jar and use it in martinis or marinades.

grazzietta's chicken liver paté

Grazzietta Chellini was my first cooking instructor in Italy. She and her family live deep in the heart of Tuscany's Chianti region, so well known for its wine. I first met this talented cook one spring evening in her beautiful garden as she was gathering herbs for our first cooking class. For several glorious days we went to her garden to gather spring vegetables, herbs, and lemons. We visited her chicken coop to gather eggs, and her hives provided us with honey for many of the dishes we completed during our stay. We were able to picnic in the vineyard where the vines were just beginning to leaf out, and we rested under the olive trees that would provide the family with olives and oil at harvest time in the fall. After my visit with the Chellinis, I felt that I had acquired many wonderful cooking skills and recipes that I am able to share with you now. This recipe is one of my favorites. Grazzietta uses pancetta when making this recipe, but I feel that bacon works equally well.

✦

CARMELA COMMENTS | You can make this pate several days ahead of serving time. If well wrapped it should be fine in the refrigerator for up to a week.

12 slices of bacon, cooked crisp and
    finely crumbled
¼ pound butter (1 stick)
1 pound chicken livers, trimmed of their fat
1 medium onion, chopped
3 shallots, chopped
½ teaspoon fresh thyme
½ teaspoon fresh rosemary
1 bay leaf
½ teaspoon salt
Freshly ground black pepper to taste
Parsley for garnish
Crostini or crackers

In a large skillet, fry the bacon and cook until crisp. Drain bacon on paper towels. Then crumble it finely and set aside. In another pan, melt the butter and add the chicken livers, onion and shallots. Stir over medium heat about 10 minutes until the livers are almost cooked through. Add the fresh herbs and bay leaf and stir frequently while cooking for 5 minutes more. Discard the bay leaf and pour the mixture into a food processor fitted with the knife blade. Add salt and pepper and process until it becomes a smooth paste. Stir the crumbled bacon into the liver mixture. After cooling, place the pate in a serving bowl and garnish with springs of thyme, rosemary or parsley. Serve with crostini or crackers.

– serves 8

marinated beef tenderloin

Beef tenderloin is my choice for Christmas Day because it is so delicious and so easy to make. I have been using this method for marinating the beef for many years, but recently changed the method for roasting. A few years ago on Christmas, I was sitting in an almost empty church with my sons, Brian and Teddy, reserving seats for the rest of the family. Behind me sat long-time friends Laurie and Bob Wehage. We started talking about our respective plans for Christmas dinner, and Bob told me about his "no-fail method" for cooking beef tenderloin. Laurie backed him up, saying it was the best method ever. I told Bob that I was going to go home and try his method out on my Christmas dinner.

Teddy, who is the real "foodie" of our family, did not think this was the time to be trying out a new method for the main course of our Christmas meal. However, I was determined to try it out, and I did. It was perfect! And it has become the method that I always use. By roasting the meat at a lower temperature for a longer period of time, I am able to enjoy my time with my company and to get dinner ready in a more leisurely way, while bringing out the best in the beef. I am hoping that you will enjoy this recipe too.

2 tablespoons black peppercorns crushed
¼ cup extra virgin olive oil
1 tablespoon cognac
2 tablespoons fresh thyme leaves, chopped
1 teaspoon kosher salt, plus more for the beef
1 whole beef tenderloin (five to six
    pounds), trimmed

Cover a baking sheet with plastic wrap, and set aside. Grind the peppercorns and transfer to a bowl. Add the extra virgin olive oil, cognac and chopped thyme leaves, and then mix well.

Spread the mixture down the middle of the baking sheet with the plastic wrap and roll the tenderloin around the marinade, making sure it is evenly coated. Wrap the tenderloin in the plastic wrap and refrigerate for a minimum of 4 hours or overnight.

Bring the tenderloin to room temperature. Preheat the oven to 225 degrees. Salt the tenderloin to taste and place it on a rack in a large roasting pan. Roast for 90 minutes or until an instant read thermometer registers 125 degrees for medium-rare.

Remove the meat from the oven and let it rest in a warm place for 15 minutes before slicing. Serve with Madeira Sauce. (See recipe on page 45.)

– serves 10-12

braised broccoli
in tomato cups

Most of this recipe can be made earlier in the day and then assembled and baked while the beef tenderloin is resting.

2 large bunches of broccoli (about 4 pounds)
8 medium tomatoes
1 cup extra virgin olive oil
2 tablespoons minced garlic
Salt and freshly ground pepper to taste

Cut the broccoli into florets with peeled, short stems. Bring salted water to a boil in a large saucepan over high heat. Add broccoli and cook uncovered until tender but crisp—about 3-5 minutes. Drain and immediately plunge the broccoli into an ice-water bath to stop the cooking process. Drain and pat dry. (This step can be done hours ahead, and the broccoli can then be refrigerated.)

Wash and core tomatoes and cut off top ⅓ of each, cutting crosswise. Carefully remove the pulp, leaving a ¼- to ½-inch thick shell. Salt and pepper the inside of the shells and invert the tomatoes on a paper towel. Set them aside and allow to drain. (Tomato cups can be prepared several hours ahead and refrigerated.)

Preheat the oven to 300 degrees. Generously butter a large baking dish. Heat the olive oil in a large skillet or sauté pan over medium high heat until the oil is hot. Remove the pan from the heat and stir in the garlic. Add broccoli and toss gently to coat. Season with salt and pepper to taste.

Arrange broccoli stem-side down in tomato cups. Set tomatoes in prepared dish. Bake just until heated through—about 7 minutes. You can arrange these cups around the sliced beef tenderloin platter if you wish.

– serves 8

Wine Pairings

With apologies to the writers of the hilarious motion picture *Sideways*, we recommend Merlot (which has fewer tannins than the Syrah or Cabernet) as the best pairing for this menu. The two domestic regions that account for most of the best Merlot are the Napa Valley of California and the wine country of eastern Washington State.

Sterling, Franciscan and Beaulieu Vineyards consistently produce good Napa Merlots. The Washington State offerings that we most enjoy are Chateau Ste. Michelle "Indian Wells" and Columbia Crest's "H-3" Merlot from the famed Horse Heaven Hills region. Anyone with the means and inclination should consider splurging on a fine Merlot for this meal from the Saint-Emilion or Pomerol districts of Bordeaux.

enza's risotto tre colore

My cousin, Enza Librandi, made this risotto mold that resembles the Italian flag for a party she and her family hosted in our honor when we were visiting them at "Casa Buona" in their vineyard in Calabria.

10 cups of chicken broth
1 stick (8 tablespoons) unsalted butter, divided
⅔ cup onion, finely minced
3 cups Arborio rice
1 cup dry white wine
⅔ cup grated Parmesan cheese
¼ cup prepared pesto
¼ cup tomato paste with Italian herbs
2 small zucchini, sliced
Extra virgin olive oil
1 clove garlic
2 fresh mozzarella balls, sliced
Salt and pepper to taste
Pam cooking spray
2 tablespoons unsalted butter

Bring the broth to a steady simmer in a saucepan on top of the stove.

Heat 6 tablespoons of butter in a heavy 5-quart pot over medium heat. Add the onion and sauté for about 2 minutes, or until it begins to soften, being careful not to burn it.

Add the rice to the pot, and using a wooden spoon, stir for one minute, making sure all the grains are well coated. Add the wine and stir until the wine is completely absorbed.

Begin adding the simmering broth to the rice, about ½ to 1 cup at a time, stirring frequently. Wait until each addition is almost completely absorbed before adding the next portion. Reserve ½ cup broth. Stir frequently to prevent sticking.

After about 18 minutes, when the rice is tender but still firm, add the reserved broth. Turn off the heat and add the remaining butter and Parmesan, stirring vigorously to combine into the rice.

Divide the risotto into 3 equal parts, using separate bowls. In the first bowl add ¼ cup pesto thinned down with a little water, and mix well. In the second bowl add the ¼ cup tomato paste thinned with a little water, and mix well. Set risotto aside.

Thinly slice the zucchini. Coat the bottom of a fry pan with olive oil. Smash 1 clove of garlic and add it to the oil, stirring until the garlic becomes golden. Remove the garlic clove and sauté the zucchini in the flavored oil. Salt and pepper them to taste and cook until they are lightly browned. Remove and drain on a paper towel.

Slice the fresh mozzarella into ¼ inch slices. Spray an angel food, bundt or ciambella pan with Pam spray. Pour the risotto with the pesto into the bottom of the pan and pack it down evenly. Layer the zucchini over the risotto. Add the plain (uncolored) risotto over the zucchini and pack it down evenly. Top this layer with the slices of mozzarella cheese. Pour the risotto with the tomato paste over the mozzarella cheese and pack the risotto down evenly. Dot the top with pats of butter. Bake in a 350 degree oven for 30 minutes. Cool slightly and unmold onto a decorative platter.

– serves 12

sicilian cassata

I have used a frozen prepared pound cake in this recipe, but you can make your own orange-flavored pound cake and then follow my directions for the filling. You can assemble this cake a few days before you serve it, making it ideal for this holiday menu.

1 large frozen pound cake, defrosted
1 pound fresh ricotta cheese
2 tablespoons of heavy cream
¼ cup sugar
3 tablespoons red and green candied
    cherries, chopped
2 ounces semi-sweet chocolate, chopped
¼ cup pistachios, chopped
3 tablespoons Grand Marnier

Put the ricotta into a large mixing bowl and beat it with the cream and sugar until it is smooth. With a rubber spatula, fold in by hand the chopped cherries, chocolate and pistachios.

Using a sharp serrated knife, slice the pound cake horizontally into 3 layers. With a pastry brush, spread the liqueur evenly over the cut slices.

Place the bottom layer of the cake on a decorative plate and carefully spread the ricotta mixture over the top. Place the center layer of cake on top and repeat, keeping the sides even. Cover with the top layer of the cake.

Gently press the loaf to make it as compact as possible, without allowing the filling to ooze from the sides. Cover the cake in plastic wrap and chill for about 12 hours.

frosting

12 ounces semi sweet chocolate, chopped
¾ cup brewed espresso coffee
½ pound unsalted butter, cut into pieces
red and green candied cherries

Melt the chocolate and the brewed coffee in a small, heavy saucepan over low heat, stirring constantly.

Take the pan from the heat. Beat in the butter, 1 piece at a time, until all the butter is incorporated and the mixture is smooth and blended.

Chill the frosting until it thickens to spreading consistency—about 30 minutes. With an offset spatula, spread the frosting over the sides and top of the loaf, in a swirling motion. Decorate the top with the cherries. Loosely cover and chill for another 12 hours.

– serves 8

Clockwise from upper left: freshly baked Italian bread, the baker's oven at Torre Melossa, produce fresh from the garden, a Prosecco mimosa, slicing prosciutto for autipasto.

MUSSELS WITH REMOULADE SAUCE

SPINACH-STUFFED MUSHROOMS

AVOCADO AND GRAPEFRUIT SALAD

CROWN ROAST OF PORK

FRUIT DRESSING

BUTTERED CARROTS

SPUMONI ICE CREAM BOMBE

In terms of entertaining, many people think New Year's Eve is the most important celebration of the year. While I do enjoy a party that evening, I really just want to spend it with a few close friends or family in a private home. You will never find us at a restaurant or at a big public celebration. The holiday for me is a time to reflect on the old year and to look forward with hope and excitement to the coming year and all that the future holds for us.

We gather at our home or at the home of close friends and share a meal together. We talk about our hopes and plans for the future. In addition, a good deal of time is spent reminiscing about the past as we watched our families grow.

The hostess sets a beautiful table using her best china, linens and silver. Everyone makes a contribution to the meal so that no one is overwhelmed with work. And, of course, there is lots of sparkling wine to drink to help make this a really special evening.

Many of the dishes for this menu can be prepared in advance, with the hosts making the main course. Ideally, we time everything so we can enjoy our dazzling dessert just as the ball drops at Time Square in New York City, and the New Year comes ringing in. And don't forget to have the Guy Lombardo CD cued up and ready to play at the stroke of midnight!

steamed mussels

Steamed mussels are one of my favorite things to eat and so easy to prepare. With the Remoulade Sauce, this provides an elegant beginning to a very special evening of celebrating the arrival of the New Year.

Make sure to buy the freshest mussels at a reputable fish market and keep them on ice until ready to prepare. Scrub the mussels well and pull out any of the beards that may remain. Steam them in a bit of wine and chill until the party begins. It is the sauce that makes this dish extra special.

6 pounds of scrubbed mussels
½ cup dry white wine
2 tablespoons finely chopped garlic
Juice of 1 lemon
½ cup minced fresh parsley

Put the mussels in a very large pot. Add the wine, chopped garlic and lemon juice to the pot. Cover the pot and place it over high heat and cook, shaking the pot occasionally. After 5 minutes, check to see if the mussels are open. Continue to cook and shake the pot until most of the mussels are open.

Remove the mussels with a slotted spoon and transfer to a large serving bowl. Discard any mussels that failed to open. Place the bowl in the refrigerator to cool the mussels. When ready to serve,

garnish the mussels with the fresh chopped parsley and serve with the Remoulade Sauce.

– serves 8

remoulade sauce

This delicious sauce recipe was given to me by the late Susan Lukens and first appeared in her cookbook, Let's Fondue! Susan was a very talented food stylist, and we worked closely together on my earlier cookbook. Susan will be remembered through her amazing work as a food stylist.

Make this sauce early in the day (or even the day before you plan to serve it) to let all of the flavors blend and develop. Place a chilled bowl of the sauce near the bowl of mussels, letting everyone garnish their own mussels with this savory cream sauce. An alternative would be to remove the mussels from *their shells and top each one with a dollop of the sauce before serving them on a beautiful platter.*

1 cup mayonnaise
1 tablespoon pickled gherkins, chopped
1 tablespoon chopped parsley
1 tablespoon capers, drained and chopped
1 teaspoon hot mustard
1 small clove garlic, minced
Hot pepper sauce to taste
1 tablespoon chopped chives

Mix all of the ingredients together except the chives. Chill thoroughly. Garnish with the chopped chives.

– makes 1¾ cups

♦

CARMELA COMMENTS | This sauce is delicious with all kinds of seafood and fish.

spinach-stuffed mushrooms

I have been making these delicious mushrooms in my cooking classes for years. They are a very healthy beginning to the decadent meal that often follows. Prepare and assemble them early in the day and then bake them just before your guests arrive.

1 (10 ounce) package frozen chopped spinach, defrosted
Small onion, chopped
¼ cup freshly grated Parmesan cheese
⅛ teaspoon salt
8 large button mushrooms
2 tablespoons extra virgin olive oil, divided

Defrost spinach and squeeze dry. Clean the mushrooms using a damp paper towel. Remove the stems and chop them. Heat 1 tablespoon of the olive oil in a pan and sauté the chopped onion until golden. Then add the chopped mushroom stems and sauté another 3 or 4 minutes. Add the chopped spinach and warm through. Remove the contents of the pan to a bowl and add the cheese, stirring this mixture well to combine. Using a pastry brush, paint the mushrooms caps with the remaining olive oil and stuff them with the mushroom/spinach mixture. Place the mushroom caps on a heatproof platter and bake them for 10 minutes in a 350 degree oven. When the stuffing and mushrooms are bubbling lightly, remove them from the oven and place them on a serving platter.

– serves 8

♦

CARMELA COMMENTS | This recipe can easily be doubled.

avocado and grapefruit salad

The Hotel Fort Des Moines was a Des Moines, Iowa, landmark. My father and I frequently ate in the hotel restaurant. I always loved a salad made with avocado and grapefruit served there and looked forward to this special lunch with my father. This version of that salad is created from my fond memories of dining in that elegant hotel.

Choose firm but ripe avocados. Slice them just before serving, assembling the salad on a Bibb lettuce leaf for an extra touch of elegance.

4 large red grapefruits
4 ripe avocados
Bibb lettuce, washed and patted dry

Using a sharp knife cut off each end of the grapefruits, leaving a flat top and bottom. Stabilize the grapefruit and peel it with the knife, making sure to cut off as much of the bitter white membrane as possible. Then cut between the membranes to separate the segments of fruit.

At serving time, arrange a large leaf of Bibb lettuce on a chilled salad plate. Place the grapefruit segments on top of the lettuce leaf. Slice the avocado and place it with the grapefruit, alternating pieces of each. Drizzle a little dressing over the top of each serving and garnish with some freshly ground black pepper.

– serves 8

poppy seed dressing

This dressing is excellent on any salad that combines lettuce and fruit.

¼ cup honey
3 tablespoons balsamic vinegar
3 tablespoons extra virgin olive oil
1 small shallot, minced
2 teaspoons Dijon mustard
1 teaspoon poppy seeds
Salt and freshly ground black pepper to taste

Add all of the ingredients and whisk together in a small bowl (or shake in a jar with a tight-fitting lid) until all of the ingredients are emulsified.

crown roast of pork

Crown Roast of Pork is an elegant entrée for this special dinner. Have the butcher prepare it for you, making sure that the roasts are of equal size.

I suggest that you prepare the fruited dressing separately in a pan. When you're ready to present the roast at table for your guests, dress it up with paper frills, arrange the dressing in the center cavity, and decorate the platter with greens and orange halves. Bring the whole platter out to present to your party and wait for the applause. Then return to the kitchen *to slice the roast and plate up the rest of the course, using the greens and oranges to decorate each plate.*

1 (8 to 10 pound) crown pork roast
2 tablespoons extra virgin olive oil
2 tablespoons Madeira wine
2 teaspoons dried thyme
2 teaspoons dried sage
4 teaspoons ground allspice
2 teaspoons kosher salt
1 teaspoon freshly ground black pepper
Salad greens
Orange halves

Early in the day mix together the extra virgin olive oil, Madeira wine, thyme, sage, allspice, salt and pepper to make a paste. Spread the paste evenly over the crown roast of pork and refrigerate.

About an hour before roasting, remove the roast from the refrigerator. Place the roast in a prepared pan or casserole. Position a rack in the lower third of a preheated 450 degree oven.

Roast at 450 degrees for 15 minutes. Reduce the oven temperature to 250 degrees and roast until a meat thermometer inserted in the thickest part of the roast registers 155 to 160 degrees.

After 1½ hours of roasting, place the pan of dressing in the oven and bake until heated through.

Remove the roast from the pan to a serving platter, reserving the pan juices. Spoon the cooked dressing into the center of the roast and cover.

Allow to rest for 15 minutes to redistribute the juices. When ready to present the roast, decorate the platter with salad greens and orange halves.

Serve slices of the crown pork roast with the reserved pan juices, dressing and buttered carrots.

– serves 10-12

Wine Pairings

The centerpiece course of roast pork with fruit dressing in this menu provides a stage for Riesling, with its consistent balance of sugar and acidity, to shine. Rieslings accommodate a wide range of other flavors. They're classified based on their relative sweetness and the maturity of the grape at the point of harvest. With the pork and fruit dressing featured here, a wine from the Kabinett or Spätlese classifications will pair beautifully.

For those who favor slightly sweeter wines, let me recommend Strub Niersteiner Patersburg Spätlese, Meulenhof Erdener Pralat Spätlese, and Trimbach Riesling from the Alsace region of France. My taste runs to slightly drier versions such as Joseph Biffar "Josephine" Kabinett "Feinherb" or Kerpen Graacher Himmelreich Kabinett "Feinherb."

Red wine enthusiasts will find that a lighter Pinot Noir will suit this menu nicely. Among the better options are Cloudline "Willamette" from Oregon and one of two California offerings—DeLoach "Russian River" and La Crema "Sonoma Coast."

fruited dressing

*T*his is a fantastic dressing that I also use at Thanksgiving. It's easy to prepare and everyone loves it. Since you're not actually stuffing it into a turkey (or, in this case, a pork roast), make it up the day before so you have less to do on the day of your party. Bake it just before serving time. I like to use apples and raisins in the dressing, but other fruit would work just as well.

8 tablespoons of butter (1 stick)
1 cup chopped celery
1 cup chopped onion
1 cup diced green apple
1 cup raisins
1 (12 ounce) bag of sage and onion stuffing mix
2 cups chicken broth

Melt butter in a large sauté pan over medium high heat. Add celery, onion, apple and raisins and cook for about 4 minutes or until soft. Remove from the heat.

Place the stuffing mix in a large bowl. Pour the vegetable and fruit mixture and warmed chicken broth over the top of the stuffing. Mix and gently toss.

Spray a large casserole with Pam or lightly butter it. Spoon the dressing into the casserole and cover with foil. Bake in a preheated 350 degree oven for 30 minutes. When ready to serve, spoon some of the dressing into the center of the roast and serve the remainder with the sliced pork.

– serves 10-12

buttered carrots

*T*his simple vegetable dish is perfect with this meal. Blanch the carrots early in the day and set them aside until you are ready to serve them. Sautéing them takes just a few minutes and can be done while the roast is resting.

2 pounds of baby carrots
4 tablespoons of sweet butter
½ cup chopped fresh parsley

In a large pot of boiling water cook carrots for 3 to 5 minutes or until they're just tender. Drain the carrots and plunge them into a bowl of ice water to stop them from cooking further and to set the color.

Just before serving, melt the butter over medium high heat in a large sauté pan. Add the carrots and sauté until they're well coated and heated through. Add the chopped parsley and toss again. Remove from the pan and serve.

– serves 8

spumoni ice cream bombe

This elegant bombe provides the perfect ending for this festive meal. Bombes were so named by the French centuries ago because the frozen dessert looked like an artillery round (or "bomb") when it was assembled. Since then, of course, the shape of real bombs has changed.

I have found that a set of nesting bowls works perfectly for this recipe. The smaller bowl can be fitted right atop the cream-lined larger bowl, assuring the evenness of the layer. One of the best things about this dessert is that it can be made ahead of time and kept in your freezer for up to a week. You can prepare one layer in the evening, let if freeze, do the second layer the next morning, and the final layer in the evening. Then decorate the whole bombe just before serving. And since it's New Year's Eve, add some sparklers to dazzle your guests and blow them right into the New Year!

1½ quarts vanilla ice cream
1 quart chocolate ice cream
1 quart strawberry ice cream
1 pint spumoni ice cream
1 cup flaked coconut
1 (10 ounce) jar Amarena cherries
Chopped pistachios for garnish

Chill a 2½-quart bowl in the freezer. Spread 1½ quarts of semi-softened vanilla ice cream around the sides of that bowl. Insert the next smaller bowl, pressing it into place to insure an even layer of ice cream. Wrap with foil and freeze.

Take this from the freezer when solidly frozen and remove the smaller bowl. Next spread a layer of chocolate ice cream within vanilla layer. Once again, insert a smaller bowl, press into place, wrap and freeze. Repeat with the strawberry layer and freeze again. Complete by packing spumoni ice cream into the center to fill the remaining hole. Wrap securely with foil and freeze until ready to serve.

To unmold, dip bowl into warm water. Loosen ice cream from bowl with a small spatula. Invert onto a chilled plate and return to the freezer until solid once again. Place in the refrigerator for 30 minutes. Remove and coat with coconut before serving. When ready to serve, turn down the lights. Add sparklers or large candles and light. Bring the bombe out to your guests to admire.

Cut the bombe into wedges and serve with a spoonful of Amarena cherries and some chopped pistachios.

– serves 8

recipe index

A

almond pear tart 112
amogio sauce 99
angel hair pasta in amogio sauce 98
asparagus, fresh-roasted 100
ANTIPASTI
    antipasti of meats, cheeses, and marinated
        vegetables 98
    antipasti skewers 80
    artichoke bruschetta 42
    bagna cauda 16
    baked stuffed brie 26
    blue cheese and honey bruschetta 105
    cannellini bean crostini 62
    caponata 68
    chicken liver paté 131
    crab salad martini 62
    crostini of sweet bell peppers 88
    goat-cheese-stuffed peppadews 130
    grazzietta's chicken liver paté 131
    jessie's goat-cheese-stuffed peppadews 130
    mushroom croustades 73
    olive bar 16
    prosciutto and melon wraps 104
    sardine spread 120
    seafood antipasto 118
    steamed mussels 140
avocado and grapefruit salad 142

B

bagna cauda 16
baked stuffed brie 26
beautiful vegetable platter 30
beefsteak wellington 28
beef tenderloin, marinated 132
berries on a cloud 48
bistecca fiorentina 64
blue cheese and honey bruschetta 105
braised broccoli in tomato cups 133
broccoli with garlic 37
buttered carrots 144

C

cannellini bean crostini 62
cannoli 101
caponata 68
carrots, buttered 144
cashew clusters 23
cauliflower salad 124
chicken in butter sauce 66
chicken liver paté, grazzietta's 131
chicken spiedini 100
chicken with prosciutto and fontina 36
chocolate-dipped strawberries 59
coconut joys 22
cod, fillet of, florentine 123
cool cucumber mint soup 72

crab salad martini 62
cranberry cake 114
cranberry relish 107
crespelle 35
crostini of sweet bell peppers 88
crown roast of pork 143

D
DESSERTS
    almond pear tart 112
    berries on a cloud 48
    bread pudding with amaretto sauce 126
    cannoli 101
    cashew clusters 23
    chocolate-dipped strawberries 59
    coconut joys 22
    cranberry cake 114
    crespelle 35
    lemon and polenta cake with fresh berries 94
    pizzelles with apricots and raspberry sauce 38
    raspberry and ginger semifreddo 76
    red, white, and blue lemon-curd tart 84
    red velvet valentine's cupcakes 31
    rhubarb crisp 69
    spumoni ice cream bombe 145
    tuscan bread pudding with amaretto sauce 126
duchess potatoes 29

E
enza's risotto tre colore 134

F
fettuccine with peas and ham 42
fillet of cod florentine 123
FISH & SEAFOOD
    cod, fillet of, florentine 123
    crab salad martini 62
    grilled salmon salad 90
    marinated shrimp skewers 17
    sardine spread 120
    seafood antipasto 118
    shrimp boil 83
    steamed mussels 140
    swordfish with pesto sauce 75
    tuna cream in phyllo cups 121
fried green tomatoes 82
frittate, vegetable (mini) 54
fruited dressing 144

G
goat-cheese-stuffed peppadews 130
grandma tursi's zucchini bread 56
granola 52
grazzietta's chicken liver paté 131
green salad with pears, walnuts and gorgonzola
    cheese 27
grilled salmon salad 90

H
herbed italian dressing 89
herbed potato salad 89

homemade granola 52

J
jessie's goat-cheese-stuffed peppadews 130

L
latin king cannoli 101
leg of lamb stuffed with spinach and mushrooms 44
lemon and polenta cake with fresh berries 94
lentil soup with spicy italian sausage 21
linguine with clam sauce 122
little flower lodge blueberry muffins 58

M
madeira sauce 45
marinated beef tenderloin 132
marinated shrimp skewers 17
marinated summer tomatoes 65
mornay sauce 123
mushroom croustades 73

O
olive bar 16
orange-brined smoked turkey 109
orange and blueberry salad 106
oranges, sliced, on a bed of arugula 124
orzo salad 68

P
parmesan dressing 47
PASTA

angel hair pasta in amogio sauce 98
fettuccine with peas and ham 42
linguine with clam sauce 122
pasta verde 76
tortellini salad in pesto 92
pasta verde 76
peppadews, jessie's goat-cheese-stuffed 130
pesto sauce 92
pizzelles with apricots and raspberry sauce 38
polenta with goat cheese and sun-dried tomatoes 34
poppy seed dressing 142
pork, crown roast of 143
potatoes, duchess 29
potatoes, sage-roasted 46
potatoes, surprise mashed 107
prosciutto and melon wraps 104

R
raspberry and ginger semifreddo 76
red, white, and blue lemon-curd tart 84
red velvet valentine's cupcakes 31
remoulade sauce 140
rhubarb crisp 69
risotto tre colore 134
roasted italian sausage 55
roasted root vegetables with balsamic vinegar 111

S
sage-roasted potatoes 46
SALADS
    avocado and grapefruit salad 142

cauliflower salad 124
green salad with pears, walnuts and gorgonzola
    cheese 27
grilled salmon salad 90
herbed potato salad 89
orange and blueberry salad 106
orzo salad 68
potato salad, herbed 89
sliced oranges on a bed of arugula 124
spinach salad with parmesan dressing 47
tortellini salad in pesto 92
vegetable salad on a bed of boston lettuce 74

SALAD DRESSING
herbed italian dressing 89
parmesan dressing 47
poppy seed dressing 142
sardine spread 120

SAUCES
amaretto sauce 126
amogio sauce 99
cranberry relish 107
madeira sauce 45
mornay sauce 123
pesto sauce 92
remoulade sauce 140
wine and mushroom sauce 29
sausage, roasted italian 55
sauteed green beans 46

SEAFOOD
crab salad martini 62
marinated shrimp skewers 17
seafood antipasto 118
shrimp boil 83
steamed mussels 140
seafood antipasto 118
shrimp boil 83
sliced oranges on a bed of arugula 124

SOUPS
cool cucumber mint soup 72
lentil soup with spicy italian sausage 21
tomato vegetable soup 20
turkey vegetable soup in mini-bread bowls 19
spinach-stuffed mushrooms 141
spinach salad with parmesan dressing 47
spumoni ice cream bombe 145
steamed mussels 140
stromboli of meat, cheese, and pesto dipping sauce
    18
surprise mashed potatoes 107
sweet bell peppers, crostini of 88
swordfish with pesto sauce 75

T
tomato-vegetable soup 20
tomatoes, fried green 82
tomatoes, marinated summer 65
tortellini salad in pesto 92
tuna cream in phyllo cups 121
turkey, orange-brined smoked 109
turkey vegetable soup in mini-bread bowls 19
tuscan bread pudding with amaretto sauce 126

V
vegetable mini-frittatas 54
vegetable salad on a bed of boston lettuce 74
VEGETABLES
    asparagus, fresh-roasted 100
    beautiful vegetable platter 30
    braised broccoli in tomato cups 133
    broccoli with garlic 37
    carrots, buttered 144
    cauliflower salad 124
    duchess potatoes 29
    fresh-roasted asparagus 100
    fried green tomatoes 82
    green beans, sauteed 46
    marinated summer tomatoes 65
    potatoes, duchess 29

potatoes, sage-roasted 46
potatoes, surprise mashed 107
root vegetables, roasted, with balsamic vinegar 111
spinach-stuffed mushrooms 141
surprise mashed potatoes 107
sweet bell peppers, crostini of 88
tomatoes, fried green 82
tomatoes, marinated summer 65
vegetable mini-frittatas 54
vegetable platter 30
vegetable salad on a bed of boston lettuce 74

W - Z
wine and mushroom sauce 29
yogurt and granola sundaes 53
zucchini bread 56

and the
celebration
continues…